# Deep Fakes

T0299867

*Deep Fakes: Algorithms and Society* focuses on the use of artificial intelligence technologies to produce fictitious photorealistic audiovisual clips that are indistinguishable from traditional video media.

For over a century, the indexical relationship of the photographic image, and its related media of film and video, to the scene of capture has served as a basis for truth claims. Historically, the iconicity of these images has featured a causal traceback to actual light rays in a particular time and space, which were fixed by chemical reactions or digital sensors to the resultant image. Today, photorealistic audiovisual media can be generated from deep learning networks that sever any connection to an actual event. Should society instantiate new regimes to manage this new challenge to our sense of reality and the traditional evidential capacities of the 'mechanical image'? How do these images generate information disorder while also providing the basis for legitimate tools used in entertainment and creative industries?

Scholars and students from many backgrounds, as well as policymakers, journalists and the general reading public, will find a multidisciplinary approach to questions posed by deep fake research from Communication, International Studies, Writing and Rhetoric.

**Michael Filimowicz** is Senior Lecturer in the School of Interactive Arts and Technology (SIAT) at Simon Fraser University. He has a background in computer-mediated communications, audiovisual production, new media art and creative writing. His research develops new multimodal display technologies and forms, exploring novel form factors across different application contexts including gaming, immersive exhibitions and simulations.

# Algorithms and Society

Series Editor:

Dr Michael Filimowicz is Senior Lecturer in the School of Interactive Arts and Technology (SIAT) at Simon Fraser University. He has a background in computer mediated communications, audiovisual production and creative technologies. His research develops new immersive media display technologies, exploring novel form factors across different application contexts including gaming, immersive exhibitions, telepresence and simulations.

As algorithms and data flows increasingly penetrate every aspect of our lives, it is imperative to develop sufficient theoretical lenses and design approaches to humanize our informatic devices and environments. At stake are the human dimensions of society which stand to lose ground to calculative efficiencies and performance, whether at the service of government, capital, criminal networks, or even a general mob concatenated in social media.

Algorithms and Society is a new series which takes a broad view of the information age. Each volume focuses on an important thematic area, from new fields such as software studies and critical code studies to more established areas of inquiry such as philosophy of technology and science and technology studies. This series aims to stay abreast of new areas of controversy and social issues as they emerge with the development of new technologies.

If you wish to submit a book proposal for the series, please contact Dr Michael Filimowicz michael_f@sfu.ca or Emily Briggs emily.briggs@tandf.co.uk

**Systemic Bias**
Algorithms and Society
*Edited by Michael Filimowicz*

**Democratic Frontiers**
Algorithms and Society
*Edited by Michael Filimowicz*

**Deep Fakes**
Algorithms and Society
*Edited by Michael Filimowicz*

For more information on the series, visit: www.routledge.com/Algorithms-and-Society/book-series/ALGRAS

# Deep Fakes

Algorithms and Society

## Edited by Michael Filimowicz

LONDON AND NEW YORK

First published 2022
by Routledge
4 Park Square, Milton Park, Abingdon, Oxon OX14 4RN

and by Routledge
605 Third Avenue, New York, NY 10158

*Routledge is an imprint of the Taylor & Francis Group, an informa business*

*British Library Cataloguing-in-Publication Data*
A catalogue record for this book is available from the British Library

*Library of Congress Cataloging-in-Publication Data*
A catalog record for this book has been requested

ISBN: 978-1-032-00260-6 (hbk)
ISBN: 978-1-032-00262-0 (pbk)
ISBN: 978-1-003-17339-7 (ebk)

DOI: 10.4324/9781003173397

Typeset in Times New Roman
by Apex CoVantage, LLC

# Contents

*List of Contributors*                                    vi
*Series Preface: Algorithms and Society*                  vii
BY MICHAEL FILIMOWICZ

*Volume Introduction*                                      x
MICHAEL FILIMOWICZ

1   **Deep Fakes: Seeing and Not Believing**              1
    SEAN MAHER

2   **Deep fakes and Disinformation in Asia**             23
    DYMPLES LEONG SUYING

3   **On the Depth of Fakeness**                          50
    EUNSONG KIM

*Index*                                                    71

# Contributors

**Eunsong Kim** is Assistant Professor in the Department of English at Northeastern University. Her forthcoming monograph *The Politics of Collecting: Property & Race in Aesthetic Formation* (under contract with Duke University Press) materializes the histories of immaterialism by examining the rise of US museums, avant-garde forms and neoliberal aesthetics to consider how race and property become foundational to modern artistic institutions. She is the recipient of the Ford Foundation Fellowship, Yale's Poynter Fellowship and a grant from the Andy Warhol Art Writers Program. In 2021 she co-founded *offshoot*, an arts space for transnational activist conversations.

**Dymples Leong Suying** is Associate Research Fellow with the Centre of Excellence for National Security (CENS) at the S. Rajaratnam School of International Studies (RSIS), Nanyang Technological University, Singapore. Her research focuses on social media, strategic communications, behavioral insights and policymaking. Her commentaries have been published in various media outlets, including Channel NewsAsia, *The Straits Times*, TODAY, *The Diplomat* and East Asia Forum. She holds a Bachelor of Business majoring in Marketing and Management from the University of Newcastle, Australia.

**Sean Maher** (PhD) is Associate Professor and the Research Training Coordinator in the School of Creative Practice at Queensland University of Technology (QUT), Brisbane, Australia. He has been recognized as Australia's lead researcher in Film and is a former president of the peak body for Australian tertiary screen education, the Australian Screen Production and Research Association (ASPERA). In 2017, he was Visiting Scholar at UCLA Film and Television Archives and prior to QUT held research positions at the Australian Film, Television and Radio School (AFTRS), Sydney, Australia, and the Communications Law Centre (University of New South Wales).

# Series Preface: Algorithms and Society

*By Michael Filimowicz*

This series is less about what algorithms are and more about how they act in the world through "eventful" (Bucher, 2018, p. 48) forms of "automated decision making" (Noble, 2018, loc. 141) which computational models are "based on choices made by fallible human beings" (O'Neil, 2016, loc. 126).

> Decisions that used to be based on human reflection are now made automatically. Software encodes thousands of rules and instructions computed in a fraction of a second.
>
> (Pasquale, 2015, loc. 189)

> If, in the industrial era, the promise of automation was to displace manual labor, in the information age it is to pre-empt agency, spontaneity, and risk: to map out possible futures before they happen so objectionable ones can be foreclosed and desirable ones selected.
>
> (Andrejevic, 2020, p. 8)

> [M]achine learning algorithms that anticipate our future propensities are seriously threatening the chances that we have to make possible alternative political futures.
>
> (Amoore, 2020, p. xi)

Algorithms, definable pragmatically as "a method for solving a problem" (Finn, 2017, loc. 408), "leap from one field to the next" (O'Neil, loc. 525). They are "*hyperobjects*: things with such broad temporal and spatial reach that they exceed the phenomenological horizon of human subjects" (Hong, 2020, p. 30). While in the main, the technological systems taken up as volume topics are design solutions to problems for which there are commercial markets, organized communities or claims of state interest, their power and ubiquity generate new problems for inquiry. The series will do its part to track this domain fluidity across its volumes and contest, through critique and investigation, their "logic of secrecy" (Pasquale, 2015, loc. 68) and "obfuscation" (loc. 144).

These new *social* (rather than strictly computational) problems that are generated can in turn be taken up by many critical, policy and speculative discourses. At their most productive, such debates can potentially alter the ethical, legal and even imaginative parameters of the environments in which the algorithms of our information architectures and infrastructures operate, as algorithmic implementations often reflect a "desire for epistemic purity, of knowledge stripped of uncertainty and human guesswork" (Hong, 2020, p. 20). The series aims to foster a general intervention in the conversation around these often "black boxed" technologies and track their pervasive effects in society.

> Contemporary algorithms are not so much transgressing settled societal norms as establishing new patterns of good and bad, new thresholds of normality and abnormality, against which actions are calibrated.
>
> (Amoore, 2020, p. 5)

Less "hot button" algorithmic topics are also of interest to the series, such as their use in the civil sphere by citizen scientists, activists and hobbyists, where there is usually not as much discursive attention. Beyond private, state and civil interests, the increasingly sophisticated technology-based activities of criminals, whether amateur or highly organized, deserve broader attention as now everyone must defend their digital identities. The information systems of companies and states conduct a general form of "ambient surveillance" (Pasquale, loc. 310), and anyone can be a target of a hacking operation.

Algorithms and Society thus aims to be an interdisciplinary series which is open to researchers from a broad range of academic backgrounds. While each volume has its defined scope, chapter contributions may come from many areas such as sociology, communications, critical legal studies, criminology, digital humanities, economics, computer science, geography, computational media and design, philosophy of technology and anthropology, along with others. Algorithms are "shaping the conditions of everyday life" (Bucher, 2018, p. 158) and operate "at the intersection of computational space, cultural systems, and human cognition" (Finn, 2017, loc. 160), so the multidisciplinary terrain is vast indeed.

Since the series is based on the shorter Routledge Focus format, it can be nimble and responsive to emerging areas of debate in fast-changing technological domains and their socio-cultural impacts.

# References

Amoore, L. (2020). *Cloud Ethics: Algorithms and the Attributes of Ourselves and Others*. Duke University Press.

Andrejevic, M. (2020). *Automated Media*. Taylor & Francis.

Bucher, T. (2018). *If . . . Then: Algorithmic Power and Politics*. Oxford University Press.

Finn, E. (2017). *What Algorithms Want: Imagination in the Age of Computing*. MIT Press. Kindle version.

Hong, S-H. (2020). *Technologies of Speculation: The Limits of Knowledge in a Data-Driven Society*. New York University Press.

Noble, S. U. (2018). *Algorithms of Oppression*. New York University Press. Kindle version.

O'Neil, C. (2016). *Weapons of Math Destruction*. Broadway Books. Kindle version.

Pasquale, F. (2015). *The Black Box Society*. Harvard University Press. Kindle version.

# Volume Introduction

*Michael Filimowicz*

For over a century, the indexical relationship of the photographic image, and its related media of film and video, to the scene of capture has served as a basis for truth claims. Historically, the iconicity of these images has featured a causal traceback to actual light rays in a particular time and space, which were fixed by chemical reactions or digital sensors to the resultant image. Today, photorealistic audiovisual media can be generated from deep learning networks which sever any connection to an actual event. Should society instantiate new regimes to manage this new challenge to our sense of reality and the traditional evidential capacities of the "mechanical image"? How do these images generate information disorder while also providing the basis for legitimate tools used in entertainment and creative industries?

Chapter 1 – "Deep Fakes: Seeing and Not Believing," by Sean Maher – provides an overview of deep fake technology with a focus on the effects on public trust in media and their significance for journalistic practices, especially in relation to fake news in the post-fact era. New forms of regulation and educational approaches to train citizens for digital literacy are discussed to counter the influence of deep fakes, which erode traditional relationships between the public and news media.

Chapter 2 – "Deep Fakes and Disinformation in Asia" by Dymples Leong Suying – analyzes deep fakes in the context of national security where they are used as elements of influence campaigns that increase strife in multi-ethnic and multi-religious populations. While the technological innovations that allow for their production cannot be curtailed, the author offers prescriptions for better enabling journalists, policymakers and the general public to become more engaged with the issues they pose.

Chapter 3 – "On the Depth of Fakeness" by Eunsong Kim – reads deep fakes against the film *Boxing Helena* to highlight how these AI-generated media are used in systems of objectification. A prominent application of this technology has been to victimize women through producing pornographic depictions, which occurs in a general legal context where the rights of those represented in media are often considered to be secondary to the rights of media producers.

## Acknowledgment

The chapter summaries here are in places drawn from the authors' chapter abstracts, the full versions of which can be found in Routledge's online reference for the volume.

# 1 Deep Fakes

## Seeing and Not Believing

*Sean Maher*

## Introduction

Deep fakes describe videos that employ artificial intelligence (AI) technology and represent false and misleading media depicting events that never occurred. By compounding the phenomenon of fake news, deep fakes underline how journalism, news and information in the digital era can be compromised. Despite being a relatively recent phenomenon, deep fakes join traditions in media representations that include hoaxes and fabrications designed as deliberate ploys to mislead and distort legitimate news and information services. Since July 2019, the specific term "deep fake" has gained currency and in conjunction with fake news constitutes part of the broader problem arising from "information disorder". Symptomatic of what has been referred to as a post-facts era, information disorder describes the effects of notions like the relativity of truth and the threats this represents to an informed citizenry and functioning polity (Anderson, 2018; Qayyum et al., 2019; Westerlund, 2019), Zannettou et al. (2019).

Deep fakes, also referred to as synthetic videos, can infiltrate news and media organizations from social media platforms through deliberate and unintended distribution. As media products, deep fakes result from layered manipulations of previous datasets harvested from video and audio sources comprising a spectrum of sound- and image-based deceptions. To understand deep fakes and differentiate them from shallow fakes, consideration needs to be given to how they are produced and the role they play in creating confusion surrounding trusted news sources.

Trust in factual data as well as the role of public institutions is connected to reliable news and information sources. Deep fakes compound the corrosive force of fake news, a term more recently conflated with criticism of legitimate information and journalism out of personal or political self-interest. Information disorder is a more encompassing notion that covers how sophisticated and malicious actors employ "computational amplification"

DOI: 10.4324/9781003173397-1

of fabricated news and data. Functioning as dis-information that manifests as deep fakes to fake social media profiles, dis-information operates by manipulating online content as well as search engine results. In a 2017 Council of Europe report, dis-information is outlined as "sowing mistrust and confusion and to sharpen existing socio-cultural divisions using nationalistic, ethnic, racial and religious tensions" (Wardle & Derakhshan, 2017, p. 1). Responding to deep fakes means locating their effects within the context of dis-information and understanding their role in compromising legitimate, fact-based information and authorized knowledge systems.

As defined by Wardle and Derakhshan, this discussion approaches deep fakes in the context of what distinguishes mis-information, dis-information and mal-information:

• Mis-information is when false information is shared, but no harm is meant.
• Dis-information is when false information is knowingly shared to cause harm.
• Mal-information is when genuine information is shared to cause harm, often by moving information designed to stay private into the public sphere.

(Wardle & Derakhshan, 2017)

By canvassing the critical response from communications scholarship, the discussion maps deep fakes in the context of information disorder and the measures being taken to ameliorate them in the evolving digital landscape and media ecology. To combat the harmful effects of information disorder, a key strategy involves the fostering of institutional resiliency, something that continues to gain currency and momentum. Notwithstanding the damaging effects deep fakes can have on specific individuals involved in their distorted representations, it is in the broader journalistic and communication domains of news and information where deep fakes may have some of the most profound effects on the broader social polity. Deep fakes have renewed calls for reforms across education and policymaking that is being marshaled to help withstand the onslaught of information disorder. By outlining these developments the discussion situates the emergence of deep fakes against the many opportunities and challenges from wider social transformations from the digital economy and information technology.

## A New Media Ecology

Polity and the public space of political thought have been redefined by a transforming communication landscape challenging the institutions of journalism and formal modes of authorized information. Disseminated from a top-down public sphere, the traditionally sober rationality of news reflected the command-and-control nature of information from mass media communications. In what is referred to as legacy media, publicly distributed information was primarily managed within the confines of a media establishment with expert communication professionals and reputable news organizations. In contrast, informal, conversational, opinion-centered communications that are often emotion-laden circulated in relatively transparent and discrete domains as nonprofessional discourse.

As the new space of media and communications continues to take shape, it is clear the former distinct spheres of communication once divided along public and private, professional and amateur, conversational and informational, rational and emotional have collapsed. Among the many transformations generated by web-based media, one of the key influences has come about from what has been described as "spreadable media" (Jenkins et al., 2013) and the rise of the amateur (Flichy, 2007). Facilitated by the ubiquity of digital affordances and propelled by social media platforms, the distributive impact of the amateur/user-generated continues to alter social, political and cultural dimensions of everyday and institutional life in the twenty-first century. The many forms of actions and interactions characteristic of online behaviors hearken to what Castells identified as the operations of "network society" – "a society whose social structure is made up of networks powered by micro-electronics-based information and communications technologies" (Castells, 2004, p. 3). The repercussions from network society on democracy are interpreted by Ferreira as "a shift from the notion of participatory democracy to that of a cooperative democracy, built 'from below' by a public that speaks without asking anybody" (Ferreira, 2016). The democratizing benefits of these shifts in communication are accompanied by the many challenges issuing from the attendant "digital disruptions" and unresolved challenges surrounding the creation and distribution of reliable information. The disintermediation of transforming supply lines of commercial activities underpinning the business models of e-commerce sees either wholesale suppliers directly linked to consumers or the number of agents between consumers and producers substantially reduced. In communication domains, however, processes of disintermediation have reduced or eliminated the role performed by publishers and news organizations as gatekeepers that contain the spread of disinformation.

As systems and processes governing the business of communications are irrevocably ceded from legacy media institutions, journalism and reliable information continue to be reconfigured against a new mediascape. While always contentious and imperfect in their relationship to news and journalism, traditional media organizations were fundamentally guided by principles of transparency, balance and accountability. As formal publishers of information, it was incumbent upon media organizations to uphold verification and authentication measures that saw them function in terms of a quality assurance mechanism. By rigorously checking the veracity of the sources of information, levels of public confidence were met by the obligations of responsible reportage that safeguarded against inauthentic news and promoted ethical responsibility.

In contrast, the phenomenon of false news coincident with the rise of social media illustrates the distributive impact of web-based and peer-to-peer-style communications. Legally constructed on different terms from publishers since the 1998 Digital Millennium Copyright Act (DMCA), internet service providers and intermediaries like social media platforms are afforded protections from liability on the legal basis of functioning as neutral hosts of user content. The marked legal and operational differences between social media platforms originating in the tech sector from traditional publishers mean operators like Facebook and Google have no editorial remit and have traditionally resisted takedown orders of user-generated content. The online media context also means the scale of content creation and those producing it have grown exponentially. Founded in 2004, in 2021 Facebook has grown to 2.74 billion monthly active users. According to Newberry, between 2014 and 2020, across Australia, Brazil, Canada, Denmark, France, Germany, Ireland, Italy, Japan, the United Kingdom and the United States, 36% of people received their news from Facebook (Newberry, 2021). Meanwhile, Google searches are estimated to be between 3.5 and 5.6 billion per day, which represents a 90% market share and provides parent company, Alphabet, with 80% of its revenue from advertising, which in 2019 totaled $US147 billion (Desjardins, 2018) and (Graham & Elias, 2021).

Reconfigured by web-based communications, the traditional media establishment and its legacy institutions not only have had to compete with firms from a rising tech sector but have also become increasingly vulnerable to being enlisted in the distribution of false and misleading news and information. Attributed to the "platformization" of newsrooms, diminished editorial oversight compromises balanced reporting. It combines with "financialization and metricization [to] push journalists and editors to produce more content, faster, and with fewer resources" (Donovan & Boyd, 2021, p. 339). The commercial dictates and 24/7 news cycle place a greater premium than ever before on "being first" and ensure traditional media organizations are forever chasing breaking news that compromises their ability to provide gatekeeping on news stories. According to Villi, "social media is the third most preferred gateway to online news, behind direct access to media outlets and almost on par with online searches" (Villi, 2019, p. 2). Traditional news media organizations have had to respond with automated social listening tools that pick up on trending stories and means of republishing them without editorial-based fact-checking.

Social media platforms and user-generated content mean the contemporary media ecology is characterized by online distribution systems that fragment news and information and diminish editorial oversight and organizational accountability. Presenting some unprecedented challenges for the global digital mediascape, the arrival of deep fakes has emphasized the need for a more concerted and robust response to information disorder. The proliferation of false news items and misleading information that manages to circulate freely online with relative impunity requires concerted intervention. There is no underestimating the scale of the challenge given that since its arrival the internet has been promoting fierce resistance at any efforts to regulate it. From tech giants to operators and users of digital currencies like Ethereum and Bitcoin, the online world still holds out utopian promises based on decentralization and the ending of state and corporate monopolies that are free of regulation. Striking a balance to support opportunities posed by the new and emerging frontiers of the virtual world with the assurances accompanying policies and enforcement of good governance remains.

## Mining Deep Fakes

Face-swap videos enabled by AI that became known as deep fakes emerged as recently as 2017. Representing a relatively new phenomenon to the suite of creations that target mis-information campaigns, deep fakes are enabled by the machine learning of AI technology. But like the many forms of fake and fraudulent communications preceding them, deep fakes are characterized by anonymous creators and the ability to capitalize on automated forms of distribution across web-based communication systems. Despite posing obvious risks, deep fake technology was ostensibly developed with benign intentions that sought to utilize large datasets of available footage that was for all intents and purposes intended for authorized usage. The AI technology beneath deep fakes is employed in legitimate applications in the film and gaming industries and can extend the kinds of virtual reality experiences sought by museums and educational media. In 2019, for example, deep fake technology facilitated an interactive experience that enabled guests at the Dali Museum in St. Petersburg, Florida, to appear to have a personal encounter with Salvadore Dali (theverge.com, Lee, May 10, 2019). Entertainment and gaming industries continue to develop and employ the technology for audio dubbing, special effects and low-cost production values that can be used to enhance high-budget and low-cost amateur productions alike.

The creation of deep fake videos requires a large dataset of publicly available video footage and audio files, then employing deep learning achieved by machines teaching themselves as machine learning models. Deep fakes are made possible by two neural networks known as generative adversarial networks (GAN) working together as the "generator" and the "discriminator". The first machine learning process, the generator, involves training on a dataset composed of a large swathe of images drawn from publicly available sites that enables it to learn and mimic a person's facial expressions and voice. The harvested images center on a target subject that includes as many face and body angles with features and expressions under multiple lighting conditions. Video forgeries are created from the data collected in this first stage of the process after swapping it onto another person by employing a deep learning algorithm. Once a video forgery has been made, its creators manually fine tune some of the results to avoid obvious image problems like glitches. The second machine learning model, the discriminator, is then employed to detect the manipulated forgeries, and only when the second model is no longer able to detect those forgeries is the deep fake complete.

At its core, the AI technology enabling deep fakes makes use of what Peter Norvig famously described as "the unreasonable effectiveness of data" and the understanding that "simple models and a lot of data trump more elaborate models with less data" (Halevy et al., 2009, pp. 8–12). The relatively simple model behind deep fakes is able to facilitate the harvesting of a large dataset of images and footage. The larger the image and footage dataset, the more equipped the machine learning models are at creating a deep fake. To date, this accounts for the proliferation of deep fakes among celebrity figures and politicians whose facial features proliferate through online images and video. GAN operates by processing hundreds if not thousands of photos of a person and being able to create a new rendering that despite the quality of the likeness is not an exact copy of any of the source images.

The scale of the threat posed by deep fakes is poised to increase as advances in AI technology mean it will be able to produce just as convincing imagery from just a few photos. Given the large amount of publicly available imagery that can be scraped from personal social media accounts, any user can become vulnerable to attacks from deep fakes. Combined with the software becoming more accessible through open source, "deep fakes in the future will likely be more and more used for revenge porn, bullying, fake video evidence in courts, political sabotage, terrorist propaganda, blackmail, market manipulation, and fake news" (Westerlund, 2019). Indeed, the harmful potential of deep fakes has already been realized from the available consumer end of software technologies, FakeApp, DeepFace Lab and audio software Respeecher used in the creation of fake videos from online pornography designed to discredit women. In 2017, these kinds of acts were escalated when an actress and investigative journalist spoke out against sexual violence and more sophisticated face-swapping AI technology was employed by anonymous fake porn creators in an act of retaliation. Uploaded to Reddit the footage soon went viral (Paris & Donovan, 2019, p. 2). Misogynistic with harmful intent, these fake videos are designed to violate women's rights and perpetuate their sexual objectification (Harwell, 2018). They can also be politically motivated, forming weaponized attacks on women who are equal rights activists spanning India to the United Kingdom.

Some of the most shared videos distorting news and political events actually constitute shallow fakes, a term used to describe audio manipulations and footage with the slightest of adjustments but significantly alter their meaning. The software for creating shallow fakes is much more widely available and requires fewer technical skill sets than deep fakes. From Adobe After Effects to free real-time filters, these applications can alter faces and slow or increase the speed of footage and produce audiovisual manipulations that while barely discernible can significantly impact public opinion. One of the most well-known cases of shallow fakes involved Congresswoman Nancy Pelosi, Speaker of the US House of Representatives. Pelosi was the target of altered videos in 2019 and again in August 2020 by using footage and audio from a press conference held in May 2020. The manipulated videos depicted Congresswoman Pelosi with slurred speech creating the impression she was intoxicated or feeble-minded. The widespread distribution of the videos represented a watershed moment in deep and shallow fakes and their pernicious role in propagating the larger phenomenon of information disorder. The effectiveness of deep and shallow fakes stems from their intention to influence attitudes and create confusion amidst the rapid flows of news and information that hinders efforts to retract and repair false and misleading impressions left in their wake.

Audio manipulations associated with deep and shallow fakes are employed to mimic voices through applications like Descript and Respeecher. Generating a spoken voice from a written text to assist podcasters, Descript advertises itself as a "collaborative audio/video editor that works like a doc. It includes transcription, a screen recorder, publishing, and some mind-bendingly useful AI tools" (www.descript.com). Rather than a simple audio-editing tool, Descript employs the AI component to seamlessly rearrange an existing recording by creating a synthetic spoken voice. Similarly, Respeecher's AI technology "combines classical digital signal processing algorithms with proprietary deep generative modelling techniques to learn your target voice inside out" (www.respeecher.com). Essentially a voice cloning product, the AI technology uses advanced audio modulation techniques to make one person's voice sound indistinguishable from someone else. Respeecher was recently employed by MIT's Center for Advanced Virtuality 2019 production, *In Event of Moon Disaster* (2019) to create the synthetic voice of Richard Nixon. In 2021 the feature documentary, *Roadrunner* employed AI audio technology to recreate the voice of its deceased subject, celebrity chef Anthony Bourdain. Reactions from the global documentary sector have questioned the ethical considerations of such a creative decision in a filmmaking format that has been defined by issues of authenticity (Sharf, 2021).

Authorized and commercial applications of AI-enabled deep and shallow fake technology reflect the innovation potential offered by such developments. It also provides the basis for arguments that technology is neutral, and it is only through usage and intent, conscious and unconscious, that applications are compromised. Such technology-agnostic perspectives support the role open-source, low-cost software available online plays in cost reduction innovations. In addition, they are seen to advance the ability to challenge existing hierarchies, power structures and hegemonic practices, and backlash on such technologies is argued to be self-serving. Social media practices in particular prompt community panic headlines by traditional media outlets aligned to the vested interests of traditional journalism. In reporting on deep fakes, a *Washington Post* headline proclaimed, "Fake Porn videos are being weaponized to harass and humiliate women: 'Everybody is a potential target'" (Harwell, 2018), heralding the technology in terms of the pending "infopocalypse." For Wahl-Jorgensen and Carlson, panic reactions from legacy media to deep fakes, "gives journalists an opening to publicly tout their professional verification practices based on their privileged claims to objective truth" (Wahl-Jorgensen & Carlson, 2021, p. 806). These perspectives argue traditional journalism has adopted a crisis mode in reporting on deep fakes because it advances positions that social media-based information is the binary opposite of traditional journalism and news. Curation, fact-checking and expert commentary get positioned as the hallmarks of traditional journalism and legacy media practices. Meanwhile, the unregulated terrain of social media and viral proclivities of web-based spreadable media gives rise to deep fakes and dis-information.

Information created, distributed and circulated across social media is rendered problematic in the face of organizations like Facebook, Google and Twitter identifying as platforms that resist the responsibilities of publishers. Traditional cautioning about legislative overreach to govern new technologies and its providers has to contend with not only the vested interests of traditional journalism and media companies but also the criminal threats posed by deep and shallow fake technologies. Extending beyond issues affecting journalism and truthful reporting of news and information, the misappropriation of AI technologies that alter video and audio has also joined the legion of threats posed by online cyberattacks. In 2019, the first reported incident involving AI-based software used to mimic a German chief executive's voice in a phone call successfully deceived an employee to transfer $US243K in corporate funds to a false account (Stupp, 2019). The criminal threats posed by deep fakes have prompted international efforts coordinated through the Centre on AI and Robotics at the United Nations Interregional Crime and Justice Research Institute, which is conducting research into technologies capable of detecting synthetic videos to counter future cyberattacks.

As recently as 2018, people were capable of detecting deep fakes through visual inconsistencies and tell-tale glitches, flickers and lighting discrepancies. But as the sophistication in AI-assisted technology proceeds apace, the explicit errors and anomalies in the creation of deep fakes are moving beyond the ability of human detection. Reponses like blockchain networks employed in conjunction with video watermarks can assist with the identification of altered and manipulated videos, while browser plug-ins like Reality Defender can alert users to suspected deep fake videos. These automated, bot-style solutions deploy algorithmic responses as a countermeasure by harnessing machine learning–assisted techniques to identify altered and manipulated videos. The "fight fire with fire" approach effectively enables algorithms to hunt down other algorithms and promises speedier identification of deep fakes before they have the opportunity to deceive unwitting users who help their circulation through sharing and reposting them.

Outsourcing detection efforts to technological measures, however, can only ever provide part of any comprehensive solution to the threats posed by deep fakes and the broader social vulnerabilities exposed by information disorder. In the first instance, clearly all technological solutions will be enhanced by the willingness by platform providers to participate in evaluating the trustworthiness of content and committing to the removal of fraudulent videos. Deep fakes used in pornography have already proven to be a catalyst in motivating platforms to be more proactive in containing the spread of malicious content. In 2018, Twitter banned deep fake–manipulated porn content from its platform after the number of tweets peaked at over 1,000, up from 65 in 2012. Of the 155 tweets containing a reference to fake porn in 2012, 65 refer specifically to involuntary fake porn. Mentions continued at similar levels until 2016, when the number of relevant tweets increased to 596 and by 2017 it was just over 1,000. In 2018, Twitter responded to the trend by banning fake porn from its platform (Maddocks, 2020).

In 2018, Gif, the provider of Gyfcat employed its Terms of Service (ToS) to ban the sharing of deep fake porn videos, and PornHub, one of the most widely used porn platforms, soon followed (Hern, 2018a). A policy reversal on deep fakes in 2018 also occurred with Reddit, the online social news aggregation and discussion board platform that in 2021 has 52 million daily registered users. In 2017, over the course of just a few months, a 90,000 member deepfake community formed using Reddit's online discussion boards, as the technology to create AI deep fakes became more user-friendly. As reported by *The Guardian* in February 2018, when the calls for taking down deepfake videos were responded to by Gif and PornHub, Reddit was initially reluctant to follow. In an abrupt pivot, however, and perhaps pressured by the response from Gif and PornHub, Reddit decided to ban its 100,000 member deep fakes community from its site. The decision was highly significant given Reddit's connection to deepfake videos since it is cited as the platform where "one user manually created the first AI-created video clips" (Hern, 2018b).

Voluntary compliance on behalf of the tech sector is a positive move in arresting the impact of deep fakes. But as legislators, social media platforms and the tech sector more widely come to terms with how instrumental digital sociality has become in daily life, the principles of good social governance will continue to clash with the ideals of unfettered free speech and the opportunity-laden possibilities generated by digital disruption. Compared to some of the strongly held positions traditionally held by a tech sector giant like Facebook, there are signs of a shift in terms of the willingness to consider more proactive interventions in areas of privacy, heightened security measures and content authentication. Following the 2016 Trump presidential election and the Brexit referendum, reconsiderations are being given to long-held positions on interventions into platform content and its amplification. In recognizing how content is neither created nor distributed equally, social media organizations have finally acknowledged how metadata manipulations and the scaling of content occur not only through investments in search engine optimization but through malicious acts spanning data breaches to calculated manipulations from engineered fraudulent accounts as well.

In 2018, irrefutable evidence of highly organized data and content manipulations was supplied by the whistleblower who revealed the data analytics firm with close associations to Donald Trump's presidential campaign, Cambridge Analytica, had accessed 50 million Facebook users without their knowledge.

The data analytics firm that worked with Donald Trump's election team and the winning Brexit campaign harvested millions of Facebook profiles of US voters, in one of the tech giant's biggest ever data breaches, and used them to build a powerful software program to predict and influence choices at the ballot box.

(Cadwalladr & Graham-Harrison, 2018)

Cambridge Analytica engaged in micro-targeting American voters through an algorithm designed to analyze individual Facebook profiles with the objective to determine personality traits, link them to swing voters and then tailor influential messaging accordingly. One month after these revelations, at Facebook's 2018 annual developer conference heightened security features were released by Facebook as part of a suite of new software products and applications, with some targeting the removal of bot-originating profiles. Facebook CEO Mark Zuckerberg used his keynote address to announce, "We have real challenges to address. . . . What I learned this year is that we have to take a broader view of our responsibility" (Kelly, May 1, 2018 CNN). The position taken by Zuckerberg in 2018 did not only seem to be a backing away from this famous maxim "move fast and break things" but was also in stark contrast to one of his longest-serving deputies, Facebook VP Andrew Bosworth. Two years earlier, on June 18, 2016, a leaked memo authored by Bosworth stated:

We connect people. Period. So we connect more people. . . . Maybe it costs someone a life by exposing someone to bullies. . . . Maybe someone dies in a terrorist attack coordinated on our tools. . . . The ugly truth is that we believe in connecting people so deeply that anything that allows us to connect more people more often is *de facto* good. . . . The best products don't win. The ones everyone use win . . . make no mistake, growth tactics are how we got here.

(Mac, Warzel & Kantrowitz, 2018)

Bosworth later recanted his comments, but similar positions were still being echoed by Sean Edgett, Acting General counsel for Twitter, during the 2017 Senate Judiciary subcommittee hearings on Russian interference in the 2016 US presidential election. Responding to a question whether he considered Twitter to be a neutral forum, Edgett responded: "Free expression and free speech is at the core of the twitter mission." In other responses to questions asking if they were in the content business, Facebook General Counsel Colin Stretch replied: "The vast majority of content on the platform is user-generated," while Google and Twitter's representatives answered in unison: "We're not in the content business" (McCarthy, 2017).

Bosworth's position and the attitudes exposed at the Senate subcommittee hearings highlighted once again the core beliefs driving the tech industry's culture. Technology is perceived as neutral, and it is only how people use it that does harm. Internet freedoms are paramount, and free speech drives popular take up that delivers profits. After 2017 these reductive views could no longer be sustained in the face of Special Counsel Robert Mueller's investigation into Russian interference in the 2016 presidential election in the United States. Mueller's report concluded that "The Russian government interfered in the 2016 presidential election in sweeping and systematic fashion" (AFP, 2019, para 1) and determined "the social media campaign and the hacking-and-dumping operations – violated U.S. criminal law" (Mueller, 2019, p. 9). These findings confirmed questions raised in the 2017 Senate Judiciary subcommittee hearings about the lack of oversight provided by Facebook, Twitter and Google. Each has been found to willingly ignore content and aggregation manipulations under the guise of free speech that has happened to favor the protection of advertising revenue. In October 2021, revelations by former Facebook data-scientist-turned-whistleblower Frances Haugen confirmed that despite its own research into the harmful effects of some of its services and products, "Facebook, over and over again, has shown it chooses profit over safety" (Ryan & King, 2021), and these latest revelations have created bipartisan calls to rein in Facebook through regulation (Allyn, 2021).

## Education and Regulation

Delivering a more secure and accountable online world requires more than holding technology companies to account. It also means promoting higher levels of general and visual literacies appropriate for our digital age. By fostering understandings of the multilayered meanings generated by images and text/image-based communications, impact from the casual consumption of online content needs to be reconfigured along lines that resemble the former expectations from word-based literacies.

Methods for distinguishing between fact and fiction that preserve creativity and innovation while still promoting free speech and privacy issues mean ensuring an informed citizenry is literate in ways appropriate to the digital era. As Silbey and Hartzog highlight,

> what we learn in the study of humanities and law is how stories work to sustain or undermine power. We might as well acknowledge this as one way deep fakes function and work from within that structure to talk back to them. Stories (fake or not) will never go away. We have to learn how to have the narrative upper hand to produce critical thinkers and win the battle for truth.
>
> (Silbey & Hartzog, 2019, p. 963)

Understanding issues of authorship and readership in terms of how producers and consumers of online content negotiate meaning-making processes from image-laden communications has become as fundamental as age-old reading and writing skill sets. Deep fakes and their inevitable unknown inheritors will continue to have unmitigated impacts until we develop educational strategies as part of a suite of responses that will help contain if not eliminate their pernicious effects. Literacies promoting understandings about the power of images means coming to terms with their inherent meaning-making properties and recognizing how fundamental they are to online communication systems.

Returning to the pioneering work of Roland Barthes and what he outlined as the "reality effect" of images ensures when photography and text are combined the image components have codified sets of data that can appear to tell the whole story. Image literacies make it clear they can only actually form part of any meaning-making structures. Barthes' pioneering work detailed the inter-relations between text and photograph, revealing a communicational core with dynamics counterintuitive to lay image literacies that have developed as a result of the innate human ability to interpret images (Peltzer, 1991, p. 24). The "reality effect" of images must be reconciled with Barthes' insight that "the photograph is not simply a product or a channel but also an object endowed with a structural autonomy" (Barthes & Heath, 1977, p. 15). This structural autonomy speaks to the relative properties of images, the awareness of which empowers consumers to be aware of the issues and limits produced by photographic verisimilitude.

The isomorphic qualities of images were seductive enough when news and information were premised on still photography. But the proliferation of video content online means there are enormous challenges when presented with casual consumers of digital media. The task of promoting semiotic understandings and differences between denotative and connotative meaning expands exponentially with the "reality effect," produced by moving images. Forming the basis of modern communications, moving imagery has ushered in what Baudrillard outlines is the wholesale displacing of reality itself. For Baudrillard, video footage has managed to achieve the kind of paradigmatic status that enables it to replace the event rather than simply represent it. In his theory of simulations, modern media has produced the phenomena where signs have come to only refer to other signs as a first order of reference rather than as a referent to reality. The result is Baudrillard's notion of hyperreality that characterizes the modern era of media. "Simulation is no longer that of a territory, a referential being or substance. It is the generation by models of a real without origin or reality: a hyperreality" (Baudrillard, 1983, p. 2).

While many critics routinely accuse Baudrillard of hyperbole as a result of misunderstanding his fatal theory of writing and communication, in the wake of accelerating distortions of reality brought about by online media practices like deep fakes, his theory of simulations strikes a renewed currency. Hyperreality results in the procession of the simulacrum that sees images constantly recombined and only referring back to themselves rather than actual events. The effect is the creation of false narratives through omissions and juxtapositions that function as coercive strategies to reinforce dominant discourses. These logics operate across a broad spectrum of meaning-making determined by images. In the context of deep and shallow fakes through to web-based circulation of imagery that propagates fake news, the implications of media simulations have perhaps never been more apparent.

> Information has a profound function of deception. It matters little what it "informs" is about, its "coverage" of events matters little since it is precisely no more than a cover: its purpose is to produce consensus by flat encephalogram. The complement of the unconditional simulacrum in the field is to train everyone in the unconditional reception of broadcast simulacra. Abolish any intelligence of the event.
>
> (Baudrillard, 1995, p. 63)

In the context of social media, the phenomenon of memes illustrates how easily digital content gets remixed and repurposed and then goes viral according to user-based web dynamics of sharing. Social media enables user-generated content as well as other content sourced

> from external sites . . . remixed into a "meme" – which has now come to mean a graphic video representation of a key moment or quote that is freed from its original context, designed to be shared, designed for impact rather than deeper dialogue or understanding.
>
> (O'Reilly, 2017, p. 205)

De-contextualized media exemplified by memes is easily re-purposed for mis-information, dis-information and mal-information because it is designed to be attention-grabbing. Often operating as clickbait, memes are indicative of how online behaviors lead to the fast and widespread distribution of content with which corrective measures have trouble keeping pace.

Against the onslaught from contemporary media production, the consumption and circulation of images online remain symptomatic of the digital era's "empire of signs." Baudrillard's theory of simulations points to how the reliance of traditional news media on images and video prepared the ground upon which web content propagating mis-communication, dis-communication and mal-information could flourish. Responding to online media's image-based communications means prioritizing digital literacies that can assist in distinguishing between reliable and unreliable information. Fragmentation and damage to consensus-based information from reliable sources produce a propensity to dismiss many items as deceptive and condemn them as fake if they challenge rather than correspond to previously held belief systems. Despite the participatory affordances of online culture as part of network society, according to Unver, "[s]ocial media has brought like-minded people closer together, but widened the gap between opposing views" (Unver, 2017, p. 1). The fracturing of mass communications into the bespoke news and information feeds of social media sees users ensconced within filter bubbles. Functioning as virtual echo chambers derived from self-selected content, these filter bubbles are only amplified by algorithmically determined derivations.

Bots and fake news fueled by algorithmic data flows contribute to the propagation of world views and political beliefs that has been described in communications scholarship as "networked feudalism." Promoting media consumption that is hyperpartisan, this leads to the kind of insular perspectives that confirms bias and is attributed to the polarization of political parties in developed and developing nations alike. From the United States and the United Kingdom to India, Brazil and Ukraine, extreme partisan politics has characterized recent elections where differences are targeted and populist leaders choose to exploit narratives of division rather than unity.

The multivalent threat of information disorder to an informed citizenship necessitates a multi-pronged approach along educational, legislative, corporate and technological lines. Despite representing only one aspect of information disorder, responses to deep fakes are symptomatic of diminishing levels of public trust and weariness of content. As Westerlund notes, "the most damaging aspect of deep fakes may not be disinformation per se, but rather how constant contact with misinformation leads people to feel that much information, including video, simply cannot be trusted" (Westerlund, 2019, p. 43). With AI-enabled deep fakes threatening to compound the effects of information disorder, the repercussions extend to a corresponding loss of faith in the public institutions underpinning liberal democracies. From a legislative standpoint, ensuring the economic gains resulting from advancements in technology that do not come at the expense of safeguarding digital democracy means finding new legal and regulatory accords with the tech sector and wider public.

Breaking down the virtual silos inhabited by digital publics means rethinking the structural components of many online business models premised on the monetizing of attention. While online engagement may form the basis of the burgeoning attention economy, in the face of the crises emerging from rising right-wing extremism to the manipulation of elections by nefarious foreign interventions, action needs to be taken that secures a digital polity for the future. The ability to broker revitalized faith in the principles of good governance means ensuring transparency and accountability across sources and providers of information. Securing and maintaining this public trust is key to regaining broader confidence in both corporate and public institutions alike.

The rise of digital media under network society has coincided with the demise of traditional media and their role as trusted gatekeepers. As a quality assurance mechanism for information, the privileged role played by traditional media as the fourth estate was accompanied by legally enforceable regulatory oversight and obligations. Often as a compensatory measure, large media organizations in the era of mass communications were afforded the protections of a restricted marketplace often through licenses that limited access to a small number of enterprises. Forming an oligopolistic marketplace, many railed at its restrictions and protections. Swept away by the open-access dynamics of the internet, the digital disruptions unleashed by web-based technologies promised a new era of pluralism in terms of sources of information and the end to concentrated media ownership. Indeed, network society with its online affordances has gone on to reorganize the fundamentals of daily social, cultural and political life. From dot-com marketplaces and digital entrepreneurship to social media's version of contemporary sociality, the online world is where, from the mundane to the sublime, everyday life now routinely plays out.

Castells saw virtual communities upholding expectations of political processes and local representation, and it was therefore a continuation of the physical and offline experience (Castells, 2011). But others like Rheingold maintain the virtual has the ability to restructure experience and politics based on its altered social relations (Rheingold, 2000). Irrespective of these competing viewpoints, however, the web and its digital domains represent ongoing recalibrations of long-standing issues of social and political life. The need for an engaged and participatory citizenry attenuated to the digital age remains premised on the foundations of reliable, trustworthy, consensus-building information.

Approaches that were developed in response to the power wielded by traditional legacy media are being adapted to the media ecology of the new online world, albeit slowly. Regulatory frameworks employed on the basis of quid pro quo benefits for all stakeholders need to be able to hold parties accountable when it comes to media and information providers that seek to influence and profit. Online content and providers of news, commentary and evolving forms of journalism may be premised on the bottom-up orientations characteristic of open-platform affordances rather than the restrictive and exclusive practices indicative of publishing and its gatekeeping functions. But enduring community values demand reliable information be based on factual data capable of standing up to verification processes. Employing the kind of technological solutions enabled by *SurSafe* and *Reality Defender*, browser plug-ins are being adapted to alert users to synthetic media (Vincent, 2018). The depiction, reporting and circulation of events that are claimed to be real will increasingly be subjected to these forms of easy and widely accessible forms of scrutiny.

The informal basis of online content saw it produced, distributed and consumed on a scale that seemed beyond any measured control capable of being supplied by the tech providers themselves, let alone by authorities pursuing enforceable regulation. Beyond the reach of national jurisdictions, the global and often anonymous basis upon which online content is created and distributed has limited the efficacy of regulatory oversight. Despite the different legal basis placed on internet service providers and social media platforms from that imposed on traditional media organizations, the past five years have seen a significant shift on the issue of the tech sector's mutual responsibility. From legislators and the consuming public to leaders in the tech sector itself, there have been moves to apply and enforce increased levels of accountability to online service providers.

Laissez-faire approaches applied to the creation, distribution and circulation of online content that were previously seen as beyond the reach of platform providers and authorities have been reconsidered. From clampdowns on copyright piracy to the dismantling of Silk Road–style marketplaces for illegal contraband, social and political will has been exercised to curtail the excesses of the previously unregulated online world. In the wake of the 2016 presidential election and the findings from the Mueller Report in 2019, major tech players like Google, Facebook, Instagram and Twitter have begun to pursue active interventions to counter malicious content exemplified by deep fakes that are either hosted or created on their platforms. Efforts like these indicate ways for remedying information disorder based on new accords that can retool fundamental journalistic standards, education and digital literacies, alongside technology solutions for verification methods.

Re-imagining regulation and its role in configuring our digital future will be key to ensuring the tech sector plays its part in dismantling the threats posed by deep fakes and information disorder. Since it is often the only means to enforce measures that go against the best interests of private firms that are deemed to compromise profits, legislation and policy frameworks have to be devised that are fit for purpose in dealing with tech giants like Google, Facebook, Amazon and Apple. In February 2021 landmark legislation was passed in Australia requiring Google and Facebook to negotiate payment deals with legacy news media institutions. Marking a global precedent, the legislation is in response to over 60% of Australians sourcing their news online, with 37.7% specifically nominating social media in 2020 (Roy Morgan, 2020). Since 2018, that level of penetration has translated into every A$100 spent in advertising in Australia – A$49 has gone to Google and A$24 to Facebook (Shayma, 2021).

Representing a mixed model of compliance, the new Australian regulation consists of voluntary and enforceable components. Despite requiring tech companies to pay for news content, the specific dollar amounts have been left up to the various parties to negotiate. Balancing levels of law making with voluntary compliance may signal paths forward for the future. Policy frameworks like this as well as government itself and how it operates need to be reimagined in our digital age. Initiatives like the Gov 2.0 Summit during the Obama administration sought new ways of governing enabled by technology as far back as 2010 (O'Reilly, 2017). Obligations as part of the social contract with the tech sector need not be confined to past adversarial approaches but rather mutually agreed-upon solutions.

> Google, Facebook, Twitter, and their like need to be understood as a new thing, which doesn't fit neatly into the old map. That new thing operates by different rules – not by whim or an unwillingness to incur the costs of curation, but by necessity.
>
> (O'Reilly, 2017, p. 203)

Combined with continued technological advancements and the fostering of digital literacies, the evolving media ecology is capable of delivering safeguards that can co-exist with innovation and reliable news and information. By updating quality assurance mechanisms once exacted by legacy media institutions, rather than seeing such responsibilities as violating dearly held principles of digital libertarianism, platform providers can safeguard standards of information to ensure the content it profits from does not come at the expense of the democratic ideals they proclaim to hold so dearly.

## Conclusion

Securing the future for life lived online means reclaiming the certainties and assurances that come from reliable, trustworthy and consensual information. As both private and public parties come together in the pursuit of the shared objectives surrounding the containment of deep fakes and broader issues of information disorder, we may find the basis for a new concord between technology and policymaking. Coordinated regulatory frameworks capable of responding to issues like deep fakes offer opportunities for new policies that can deliver tangible and measurable benefits. Future policy cannot function or be framed based on the dynamics of legacy media. Instead, just as a policy and measures like journalistic standards developed over time to contain the influence of legacy media in the twentieth century, new approaches have to be repurposed for the enormous challenges posed by online and AI technologies.

In an age of uncertainty, nothing may prove as harmful to a society predicated on information as that arising from its negative dialectics – dis-information, mis-information and mal-information. When it comes to technology-based solutions to deep fakes, the vaccine logic appears likely to be one effective strategy by using algorithms to fight algorithms for effective authentication measures. In terms of employing education, it means embracing digital literacies and retooling the three "R"s appropriate to the audiovisual mediascape of the internet era. Corporate responsibility has perhaps one of the largest roles to play, one that combines legal and voluntary compliance premised on mutual obligations that accompany the enormous influence wielded by technology companies and their services. The coordination of these multi-pronged responses involving technology, education and corporate governance will not just contain information disorder today but can restore institutional resilience to equip us for the future tumults erupting from network society.

## References

AFP. (2019). *Main Point of Mueller Report*. https://web.archive.org/web/20190420143436/www.afp.com/en/news/15/main-points-mueller-report-doc-1fr5vv1

Allyn, B. (2021). Here are 4 Key Points from the Facebook Whistleblower's Testimony on Capitol Hill. *NPR Online*. www.npr.org/2021/10/05/1043377310/Facebook-whistleblower-frances-haugen-congress

Anderson, K. E. (2018). Getting Acquainted with Social Networks and Apps: Combating Fake News on Social Media. *Library HiTech News*, 35(3), 1–6.

Barthes, R., & Heath, S. (1977). *Image, Music, Text*. Fontana.

Baudrillard, J. (1983). *Simulations*. Semiotext[e].

Baudrillard, J. (1995). *The Gulf War Did Not Take Place*. Indiana University Press.

Cadwalladr, C., & Graham-Harrison, E. (2018). Revealed: 50 Million Facebook Profiles Harvested for Cambridge Analytica in Major Data Breach. *The Guardian*. www.theguardian.com/news/2018/mar/17/cambridge-analytica-Facebook-influence-us-election

Castells, M. (2004). Informationalism, Networks, and the Network Society: A Theoretical Blueprint. In Castells, M. (ed.), *The Network Society. A Cross-Cultural Perspective*. Edward Elgar Publishing Ltd, pp. 3–45.

Castells, M. (2011). *The Rise of the Network Society: The Information Age: Economy, Society, and Culture*. John Wiley & Sons.

20  *Sean Maher*

Desjardins, J. (2018). How Google Retains More Than 90 Percent of Market Share. *Business Insider*. www.businessinsider.com/how-google-retains-more-than-90-of-market-share-2018-4

Donovan, J., & Boyd, D. (2021). Stop the Presses? Moving From Strategic Silence to Strategic Amplification in a Networked Media Ecosystem. *The American Behavioral Scientist* (Beverly Hills), 65(2), 333–350. https://doi.org/10.1177/0002764219878229

Ferreira, G. M. (2016). In Search of a Return to Communication (Studies) as a Factor of Social Change: Web 2.0 and Political Participation. In Goncì§alves, G., Serra, J. P., & Dahlgreen, P. (eds.), *Politics and Web 2.0: The Participation Gap*. Vernon Press, pp. 13–26.

Flichy, P. (2007). *The Internet Imaginaire*. MIT Press.

Graham, M., & Elias, J. (2021). How Google's $150 billion Advertising Business Works. *CNBC.com*. www.cnbc.com/2021/05/18/how-does-google-make-money-advertising-business-breakdown-.html

Halevy, A., Norvig, P., & Pereira, F. (2009, March–April). The Unreasonable Effectiveness of Data. *IEEE Intelligent Systems*, 24(2), 8–12.

Harwell, D. (2018, December 30). *Fake Porn Videos are being Weaponized to Harass and Humiliate Women: 'Everybody is a Potential Target'*. www.washingtonpost.com/technology/2018/12/30/fake-porn-videos-are-being-weaponized-harass-humiliate-women-everybody-is-potential-target/ (accessed 29 July 2021).

Hern, A. (2018a, February 7). *The Guardian.com*. www.theguardian.com/technology/2018/feb/07/twitter-pornhub-ban-deepfake-ai-face-swap-porn-videos-celebrities-gfycat-reddit (accessed 11 May 2021).

Hern, A. (2018b, February 8). *The Guardian.com*. www.theguardian.com/technology/2018/feb/08/reddit-bans-deepfakes-face-swap-porn-community (accessed 11 May 2021).

Jenkins, H., Ford, S., & Green, J. (2013). *Spreadable Media: Creating Value and Meaning in a Networked Culture*. New York University Press.

Kelly, H. (2018). Facebook Tries to Move Past Scandals with New Features. *CNN.com*. https://money.cnn.com/2018/05/01/technology/Facebook-f8-2018-zuckerberg-keynote/index.html?iid=EL

Lee, D. (2019). Deepfake Salvadore Dali Takes Selfies with Museum Visitors. *The Verge*. www.theverge.com/2019/5/10/18540953/salvador-dali-lives-deepfake-museum

Mac, R., Warzel, C., & Kantrowitz, A. (2018). Growth at Any Cost: Top Facebook Executive Defended Data Collection in 2016 Memo – and Warned That Facebook Could Get People Killed. *BuzzFeednews*. www.buzzfeednews.com/article/ryanmac/growth-at-any-cost-top-Facebook-executive-defended-data

Maddocks, S. (2020). "A Deepfake Porn Plot Intended to Silence Me": Exploring Continuities between Pornographic and "Political" Deep Fakes. *Porn Studies* (Abingdon, UK), 415–423. https://doi.org/10.1080/23268743.2020.1757499

McCarthy, T. (2017). Facebook, Google and Twitter Grilled by Congress over Russian Meddling – as it Happened. *The Guardian*. www.theguardian.com/technology/live/2017/oct/31/Facebook-google-twitter-congress-russian-election-meddling-live (accessed 9 July 2021).

Mueller, R. (2019). *Report on the Investigation into Russian Interference in the 2016 Presidential Election* (Vol. I). www.justice.gov/archives/sco/file/1373816/download

Newberry, C. (2021). 47 Facebook Stats That Matter to Marketers in 2021. *Hootsuite. com.* https://blog.hootsuite.com/Facebook-statistics/#General_Facebook_stats

O'Reilly, T. (2017). *WTF? What's the Future and Why It's Up to Us.* Penguin and Random House.

Paris, B., & Donovan, J. (2019, September 18). Deepfakes and Cheap Fakes. *Data & Society.*

Peltzer, G. (1991). *Iconographic Journalism.* Rialp Editions.

Qayyum, A., Qadir, J., Janjua, M. U., & Sher, F. (2019). Using Blockchain to Rein in the New Post-Truth World and Check the Spread of Fake News. *IT Professional,* 21(4), 16–24. https://doi.org/10.1109/MITP.2019.2910503

Respeecher. *Voice Cloning Product Powered by Artificial Intelligence.* www.respeecher.com/product

Rheingold, H. (2000). *The Virtual Community: Homesteading on the Electronic Frontier.* MIT Press.

Roy Morgan Research. (2020). *It's Official: Internet is Australia's Main Source of News; TV Remains Most Trusted.* www.roymorgan.com/findings/8492-main-sources-news-trust-june-2020-202008170619

Ryan, M., & King, C. (2021). Whistle-Blower says Facebook Chooses Profits over Safety. *New York Times.* www.nytimes.com/2021/10/03/technology/whistle-blower-facebook-frances-haugen.html

Sharf, Z. (2021). Anthony Bourdain Doc Recreates His Voice Using Artificial Intelligence and 10-Plus Hours of Audio. *Indiewire.* www.indiewire.com/2021/07/anthony-bourdain-doc-artificial-intelligence-recreate-voice-1234651491/?fbclid=IwAR2UYxuN2oIVCiQ0cPOWuzycvQzw1HbKWufvgr-EdjuyVkcsLwd713T1pLI

Shayma, K. (2021). Facebook and Google News Law Passed in Australia. *BBC.com.* www.bbc.com/news/world-australia-56163550

Silbey, J., & Hartzog, W. (2019). The Upside of Deep Fakes. *Maryland Law Review,* 78(4), 960–966.

Stupp, C. (2019). Fraudsters Used AI to Mimic CEO's Voice in Unusual Cybercrime Case. *The Wall Street Journal.* www.wsj.com/articles/fraudsters-use-ai-to-mimic-ceos-voice-in-unusual-cybercrime-case-11567157402

Unver, H. A. (2017). Digital Challenges to Democracy: Politics of Automation, Attention, and Engagement. *Journal of International Affairs* (New York), 71(1), 127–146.

Villi, M. (2019). Social Media as Distribution Tool. In Vos, T. P., Hanusch, F., Dimitrakopoulou, D., Geertsema-Sligh, M., & Sehl, A. (eds.), *The International Encyclopedia of Journalism Studies.* https://doi-org.ezp01.library.qut.edu.au/10.1002/9781118841570.iejs0184

Vincent, J. (2018). Browser Plug-Ins That Spot Fake News Show the Difficulty of Tackling the Information Apocalypse. *The Verge.* www.theverge.com/2018/8/23/17383912/fake-news-browser-plug-ins-ai-information-apocalypse

Wahl-Jorgensen, K., & Carlson, M. (2021). Conjecturing Fearful Futures: Journalistic Discourses on Deepfakes. *Journalism Practice*, 15(6), 803–820. https://doi.org/10.1080/17512786.2021.1908838

Wardle, C., & Derakhshan, H. (2017). *Information Disorder: Toward an Interdisciplinary Framework Research and Policy Making* (No. 9). Council of Europe.

Westerlund, M. (2019). The Emergence of Deepfake Technology: A Review. *Technology Innovation Management Review*, 9(11), 40–53.

Zannettou, S., Sirivianos, M., Blackburn, J., & Kourtellis, N. (2019). The Web of False Information: Rumors, Fake News, Hoaxes, Clickbait, and Various Other Shenanigans. *Journal of Data and Information Quality*, 1(3), Article No. 10. https://doi.org/10.1145/3309699

# 2 Deep fakes and Disinformation in Asia

*Dymples Leong Suying*

## Introduction

In February 2021, users of the popular social media application TikTok were amused to see videos of actor Tom Cruise playing golf and practicing magic tricks. It was later revealed that the Tom Cruise in the videos was in fact not the *actual* Tom Cruise but a deepfake. The highly realistic deepfake astounded viewers and led people to a bewildering dilemma: can we really believe what we see online?

Technology has expanded at a rapid pace. AI capabilities can now create synthetic media – the generation of artificial images, video and audio – at a highly realistic level (GRC World Forums, 2021). This hyperrealism recalls the notion of the uncanny valley, where AI-generated content seems indistinguishable from actual humans. Although machine learning has been around since 2014, public visibility has increased in 2019, with thispersondoesnotexist.com, a website that generates fake faces. A greater awareness of deep fakes has exploded into the public arena, from the creation of non-consensual images of women to concerns over the potential weaponization of deep fakes in global elections. The potential deployment of deep fakes for influence operations – the coordinated effort to manipulate public debate – has further amplified debate over the use of deep fakes as vectors of disinformation (Facebook, 2021). The challenges brought by the COVID-19 pandemic have provided fertile ground for disinformation and misinformation to grow.[1] The gradual ubiquitousness of deep fakes and synthetic media will result in a paradigm shift in how we think about information creation and dissemination in the digital information space.

This chapter examines the role of deep fakes – its origins, history, uses and nature as a tool for disinformation. It explores the issues associated with its deployment for disinformation in Asia and looks at future trends. Potential prescriptions to address the concerns brought about by deep fakes are also explored.

DOI: 10.4324/9781003173397-2

## What Are Deep fakes

Deep fakes are a category of synthetic media and are either *wholly generated or manipulated* by AI. Deep fakes can consist of videos, images and audio, or a combination of the three, and are generated using a specific form of AI known as deep learning (Sample, 2020).

Deep learning, a subcategory of machine learning in which algorithms learn and acquire experience without human involvement, utilizes artificial neural networks, which processes large amounts of data for decision-making. The training of neural networks – a series of algorithms modeled after the neurons in the human brain – can recognize the underlying relationships existing in data. The system constantly adapts its structure to information that flows through multiple layers of learning – hence the word "deep." Deep learning enables machines to solve complex problems using a diverse and unstructured dataset. For instance, the creation of a deepfake image of a person would entail having hours of real video footage of an individual to enable a realistic comprehension of what a person looks like from various angles and lighting. Trained networks are then combined with computer-graphic techniques to superimpose a copy of the person onto a different actor (Mirsky & Lee, 2021). The image is constantly tweaked and improved to remove obvious cues of synthetic manipulation for the image to be believable while algorithms constantly learn through understanding patterns and improve on more data.

Deep fakes can be categorized into three types of synthesized media (Agarwal et al., 2019), namely:

(1) face-swap, where a face in a video is automatically replaced with another. Inserting famous actors into movie clips which they have never acted in, for instance, is an example of a common category of synthesized media seen on social media and the internet.
(2) lip-sync, whereby the mouth region of a person in a video is manipulated to "match" an audio recording, as seen in the Barack Obama deepfake created by actor Jordan Peele and Buzzfeed (Vincent, 2018a).
(3) puppet-master, in which a performer acts out movements and expressions of a target person; akin to using a Tom Cruise impersonator for a deepfake video (Kahn, 2021b).

The inclusion of generative adversarial networks (GANs), a class of deep learning algorithms, can generate an even higher level of realistic content. GANs are categorized as neural networks that compete and duel against the other to generate new data – hence, the name "adversarial" – and improve on the output of the other, with one network (the discriminator) trained to detect real images and videos and the other network (the generator) learning over time to produce outputs to deceive detection. Thus, GAN-generated images are almost close to perfectly resembling or are representative of how actual human beings look.

The website thispersondoesnotexist.com is a good example of how far GANs have come into the generation of realistic synthetic images. However, the creation of GANs requires a huge amount of data to be successful and highly skilled expertise (Adee, 2020). Most deep fakes are generated by deep learning algorithms where the inclusion of GANs does not play a prominent role and is a combination of AI and non-AI algorithms.

## The Rise of Deep fakes

The term "deepfake" was first coined by a user named "Deep fakes" on the popular discussion platform Reddit – a combination of the words "deep learning" and "fake." The user had uploaded videos whereby the faces of popular celebrities such as Gal Gadot were swapped onto the bodies of pornographic actors and posted online on the subreddit "r/deep fakes" (Cole, 2018). Trained on images of various celebrities gathered from Google and YouTube, the AI algorithm learnt to swap faces of celebrities frame by frame into an existing porn video. While "r/deep fakes" was ultimately shut down by Reddit, the tools and techniques for face-swapping were freely shared online (Robertson, 2018) and have steadily crept into mainstream social media platforms. Research revealed that deepfake pornographic videos accounted for 96% of all deepfake videos online in 2019, despite the rise in non-pornographic deepfake videos (Adjer et al., 2019).

Deep fakes have gone beyond targeting celebrities. Ordinary individuals have become victims of fake pornography campaigns, where publicly available photos taken from social media accounts are manipulated. The proliferation of apps and providers offering to alter images of women as nude have also increased in recent years (Cole, 2019). Research showed that such services offer opportunities for the anonymous submission of photos to receive altered nudes in return (Harwell, 2020). With one click of a button an image of a woman is synthetically stripped for the purposes of pornography, and images are shared within forums or chat groups and shared on platforms such as Telegram (Solsman, 2020). Some services even offer paid premium exclusive services such as the removal of watermarks on fake nudes and the caching of photos on a hidden channel (Harwell, 2020). The creation of fake nudes can be insidious as any woman can unknowingly be a victim, when having a mere online presence on social media or the internet creates vulnerabilities for potential attack, creating opportunities for revenge porn and blackmail.

Deep fakes have also been used for cybercrime. Cybercriminals allegedly used a deepfake audio to impersonate a CEO (Stupp, 2019), and a father was scammed of money when an alleged deepfake audio was used to impersonate his son (Rushing, 2020). Deepfake fraud is among the ways in which AI can be used for crime – making it harder for people to trust what they see online, further emphasizing the need for greater ID verification processes.

Criticism has led some to call for the banning of deep fakes due to the threats presented in the safeguarding of public security and safety. Deep fakes, however, are not all malicious and can be positive.

While deep fakes can be deployed for malicious and criminal purposes, synthetic media promises to enhance benefits. The increase of synthetic media for legitimate commercial purposes such as entertainment and video production reveals the potential for individuals to produce a Hollywood production-style movie on a laptop in the future. This democratization of technology can also allow content creators to produce high-fidelity simulations of the real world and unlock powerful benefits for creative industries. Synthetic media technology also promises to provide transformational impact toward industries such as advertising, education and marketing. For instance, David Beckham's deepfake educational video calling on the world to end malaria allowed audiences from various countries to hear the appeal in their own native language (Reuters, 2019b). K-pop virtual idols have also been produced, complete with individual characteristics, voices and personalities – joining the burgeoning list of AI-created celebrities in South Korea (Sng, 2021). Video production can be scalable and powered by AI, dramatically reducing the process of video production and the amount of time, effort and cost involved. Synthetic media is reshaping commerce and communications and could unleash greater levels of creativity and communication in commercial industries.

A blanket ban on deep fakes would be impractical to enforce due to the anonymity of a borderless internet (Toews, 2020). Furthermore, such a ban would also present constitutional challenges in certain countries, such as the United States (Sunstein, 2021). A combination of both legislation and regulation for deep fakes has been/is considered being used in countries to regulate deep fakes.

## What Makes Deep fakes Impactful?

Deep fakes have a more direct effect on the psychology of the audience compared to other types of media (Minsky, 2021). Videos – being more visceral in nature as a more direct form of representation of reality – are highly influential in helping people understand and learn information (Kemp, 2020).

While human cognition predisposes us to be influenced by visual and audio evidence, it is especially so when the quality of video or audio is questionable to the extent that our eyes and ears cannot accurately decipher the artificialness of the content (Vaccari & Chadwick, 2020).

Humans are primed to believe something that looks and sounds right – a cognitive bias called processing fluency, which refers to the unconscious bias in favor of information that our brain can process quickly (Schick, 2020). Our heuristic biases impact the receptivity to deep fakes and are more believable when it aligns with existing viewpoints or pre-held notions of the viewer (Chesney et al., 2020). Deep fakes of well-known public figures, such as celebrities and politicians, highlight the realism heuristic, where the believability and trust of visual information are preferred. This leads to a higher propensity for misleading visual content to generate false perceptions, as individuals tend to view images and audio as a greater accurate depiction of how the "real world" is experienced. A good example includes the hyperrealistic deep fakes of Tom Cruise on TikTok, which has bewildered audiences on the platform and has gained millions of views (CNN, 2021). The familiarity which viewers with the actor and his mannerisms led some to believe that the deepfake was the actor himself. The technical realism of similar deep fakes intensifies the issue that fluency can be generated through familiarity (Vaccari & Chadwick, 2020) and can impede the ability of audiences to enable the formation of legitimate informed decisions (Diakopoulos & Johnson, 2020).

## The Marriage of Deep fakes and Disinformation

The deployment of deep fakes in influence campaigns has been of particular concern. Deep fakes have the potential to further fragment and amplify societal divergences, and can be used to potentially instigate unrest, confusion and even violence. Deep fakes created for the purpose of disinformation could potentially incite physical mobilizations and could result in violence and a potential threat toward public safety and national security (BBC, 2019). The unease over the deployment of deep fakes to influence elections has raised concerns globally over its potential weaponization against free and fair elections. In the backdrop of this information environment, deep fakes have the potential to destabilize countries and influence elections by spreading disinformation.

Cases of deep fakes have been deployed in disinformation campaigns. In 2019, Facebook removed a coordinated inauthentic network of 900 pages, and accounts were managed mainly out of Vietnam. The network was linked to the Epoch Media Group, a far-right US-based media grouping known to engage in misinformation tactics (Hao, 2021). While some fake accounts utilized profile photos taken from the internet, most accounts identified utilized fake profile photos generated by AI (Venkataramakrishnan, 2020). These "new" personas were created using GANs and were given identities to create inauthentic accounts on Facebook, masquerading as Americans on Facebook groups (Nimmo et al., 2019). The influence campaign was the "first large-scale deployment of fake faces" on social media (ibid). The campaign is a flashpoint for how future disinformation campaigns could be conducted – using a combination of disinformation strategies, such as coordinated inauthentic accounts and deep fakes – on a wider, global scale.

The usage of deepfake images as profile photos is unfortunately not novel. An investigation in 2019 revealed a fake LinkedIn profile of Katie Jones, whose profile featured a GAN-generated deepfake. The Katie Jones profile had connected with prominent researchers and academics worldwide from prominent think tanks. The investigation revealed that such efforts had the hallmarks of a state-run operation. Espionage efforts on the popular networking platform have led governments such as France and Germany to issue warnings on being approached on LinkedIn (Satter, 2019). British intelligence agency MI5 has also cautioned its employees on the potential for such social engineering techniques using AI (Corera, 2021).

A similar strategy was used in a June 2020 information operation involving the creation of a network of fake journalist and political consultant personas (Rawnsley, 2020). Hyperrealistic deep fakes were used in tandem with fake journalist identities to write political articles for conservative publications online. Reporting revealed another instance of fake journalist personas involving deepfake technology (Satter, 2020). Editors of various news outlets in which articles were published admitted that they did not thoroughly vet the identities of the fake journalists and their articles. While attribution for the disinformation campaign could not be established, forensic detection technology conducted by deepfake analysis experts determined that the photographs had characteristics of deep fakes. Profile pictures using deepfake technology adds an additional layer of protection to hide the identity of the operator of the campaign as the pictures cannot be debunked using reverse imaging (Vincent, 2019). This is a salient reminder of the ease with which widespread disinformation efforts can spread when operators are able to mask their identities behind deepfake-generated personas to spread disinformation online (Satter, 2020).

The usage of synthetic media in disinformation operations could become threat vectors in the coming future. In March 2021, the Federal Bureau of Investigation (FBI) warned in its threat assessment report that the usage of synthetic content for cyber and foreign influence operations would be leveraged by malicious actors. The assessment report further stated that influence operations utilizing GAN-generated synthetic profile images were of specific concern (Federal Bureau of Investigation, 2021).

Deep fakes remain a disruptive force to authenticity in the digital age. The issue of authentic videos being dismissed as fake is a potential threat. When authenticity is either lost or cannot be confirmed, it threatens to undermine the whole media ecosystem, where the ability to discern authenticity is crucial. Allegations of manipulation of authentic videos have already damaged legitimacy and reputations (Hao, 2019). An example of this occurred when a video of President Ali Bongo of Gabon sparked an unsuccessful military coup whereby the mere notion of alleged inauthenticity of the video – his political rivals alleged the video of being a deepfake – was enough to amplify the confusion and mistrust of the people and led to the conclusion that there was some form of conspiracy at work (Breland, 2019).

This is a clear example of the liar's dividend. Chesney and Citron (2018) state that deep fakes promote the notion of the liar's dividend – convincing others that fictional things happen and avoiding accountability for things that are true, and in doing so, sow doubt on the authenticity of a deepfake. The danger is in the fact that deep fakes can be used to create doubt about the content of real videos, by alleging that they could be manipulated, in which reality becomes deniable. The audience could be thus primed to be skeptical of real video evidence certified by experts. Public uncertainty regarding the authenticity and truthfulness of content could be eroded and also result in diminishing levels of public trust in news (Vaccari & Chadwick, 2020). This leaves the onus of verification on the audience and places a huge amount of cognitive taxation to authenticate informational content.

## Deep fakes and Disinformation in Asia

Deepfake activity is growing in Asia. Asia has seen incidences of deepfake images of women celebrities in the region. Research notes that individuals in South Korea, India and Japan have made up a significant proportion of targets (Adjer et al., 2019). In South Korea, for instance, a spate of illegal deepfake images of celebrities resulted in a petition against deep fakes (Ryall, 2021). Cybercriminals have targeted women online in Japan, amidst a rise in sex-related cybercrime (Ryall, 2020). Deepfake applications such as FaceApp and Zao, while predominantly used for entertainment purposes, were abused by others. Deep Nude was used by Indian cybercriminals to generate nude pictures of women by obtaining photos through social media accounts, and these pictures were used for blackmail, extortion, revenge porn and character assassination (Mengle, 2020).

The usage of deep fakes for political purposes has also occurred in Asia. The first instance of the deployment of a deepfake for a political campaign in India occurred during the 2020 Legislative Assembly elections in India (Christopher, 2020). Manipulated videos of Bharatiya Janata Party (BJP) President Manoj Tiwari were distributed across 5,700 WhatsApp groups in Delhi and the surrounding areas, reaching around 15 million people in India.[2] The increase in deep fakes, aided by the growing number of tools and services in India, has made it easy for non-experts to create deep fakes. Deepfake videos have also been used to smear the reputation of women politicians and journalists in India. Chandrani Murmu, the youngest Indian Member of Parliament, was the target of a deepfake video, where her face was superimposed onto an obscene video ahead of her election in 2019 (Mackintosh & Gupta, 2020). In 2018, Indian journalist Rana Ayyub was targeted in a deepfake pornographic video amid an influence campaign on Twitter and WhatsApp (Ayyub, 2018).

AI-generated faces have been used in coordinated influence campaigns allegedly originating from Asia. In 2020, Facebook took down a network of fake accounts originating in China which was spreading government propaganda on the platform (Facebook, 2020b). While there was a small amount of activity directed at the 2020 US election, most of the identified efforts were directed toward efforts to promote pro-China interests and narratives in Southeast Asia, specifically in the Philippines and the South China Sea. Investigations also revealed the usage of GAN-generated faces in efforts to disguise fake accounts – an increasingly prevalent technique used in information operations globally (Nimmo et al., 2020). Further investigations revealed a network of an inauthentic cluster of 14 Twitter accounts utilizing GAN-generated faces as profile pictures promoting Chinese 5G capabilities in Belgium (Graphika, 2021). The usage of GAN-generated faces removes the need for using pilfered profile pictures to disguise fake accounts, avoiding risk of detection by traditional investigative techniques such as reverse image search. While GAN-generated images are currently still limited, the images may look realistic to the untrained eye.

Deepfake videos have also been used in Southeast Asian countries. The issue of deep fakes was brought to the forefront of Malaysian public discourse in 2019 when a video allegedly involving a senior cabinet minister and a former private secretary to a deputy minister engaging in sexual acts was circulated on WhatsApp, subsequently going viral on social media. Investigations revealed the video to be authentic. Foreign digital forensic experts further verified the video was not digitally altered (Boo, 2019). However, the investigations and facial recognition analysis could not confirm or determine that the Minister was in the video. Police investigations further stated that the video was masterminded by a leader of a political party, and the parties involved were hired to produce and distribute the video (Reuters, 2019c). The ambiguity and lingering doubt had served to amplify increasingly combative vitriol online among various political and public factions. The controversy serves to illustrate how the mere suspicion or doubt of alleged deep fakes undercuts public trust toward institutions and media agencies, and damages the authenticity and factual accuracy of news reporting – an example of the liar's dividend – in which a distrustful public remains skeptical over conflicting statements of authenticity over the video.

## Current Trends

### *Increasing Commercialization of Synthetic Media Apps and Services*

Synthetic media capabilities have increasingly been commercialized as technologies in relation to face-swapping and image translation are more accessible. Commercial products are being built to make synthetic media a part of everyday lives. As the barriers in which synthetic media are generated decrease over the years, the future might see deep fakes becoming easier and cheaper to produce, thus increasing its commercial viability (Burgess, 2020).

The commercial application of synthetic media will be a growing trend due to the popularity of such applications on social media and the internet. Professional services offering synthetic media technologies and capabilities will also expand to cater to a niche but growing demand for quality synthetic media for advertising and marketing purposes. Content generated via such apps allow for meme-ification, whereby users can mash together public figures, characters and songs, and this is usually highly viral on social media (Vincent, 2021). Popular synthetic media apps, once considered novel, are now prevalent. These apps are making it easier to make AI-powered manipulated videos and share them across social media. Asia has seen a rapid growth in the usage of digital technology and social media and a proliferation in the number of mobile apps in the region among Asian populations. This could be a fertile landscape for the proliferation of deepfake generation and consumption –for both entertainment and creative purposes – and the potential of deep fakes for disinformation purposes to thrive.

### *Deep fakes and Disinformation for Sale*

Global "disinformation for hire" services are available (Bradshaw & Howard, 2019). In recent years, influence operations conducted by commercial actors – offering a whole suite of services such as media, marketing and public relations – have been identified in countries such as Myanmar, the United States, the Philippines, Ukraine, Egypt and the UAE. Worldwide, politicians, parties, governments and others hire "black PR" firms to manipulate online discourse (Silverman et al., 2020). Commercial operations offer influence operations services to clients both at home and abroad, allowing them to leverage services to run their own campaigns (Facebook, 2021). In the long run, as synthetic media technologies improve and increase, the generation of advanced high-quality deep fakes for the purposes of disinformation for political purposes could occur. These could become key tools for propagandists worldwide, as countries with advanced AI capabilities and access to large data troves can gain advantages in information warfare. The future could see the rise of information operations for hire, in which deep fakes are but part of the disinformation toolbox for sale, where parties mounting a disinformation campaign replete with a whole suite of tools, and deep fakes could be layered into propaganda campaigns to improve its effectiveness. Deepfake generation could be just one of the additional services offered as deepfake as a service.

## Shallowfakes in Asia: A More Pressing Concern

The threat of deep fakes has the potential to exacerbate the spread and intensity of disinformation in Asia. Deep fakes as a propaganda technique for influence campaigns are not prevalent in Asia, in part due to technical obstacles to deepfake creation and detection. Most misinformation and disinformation efforts that have been perpetuated globally – specifically in Asia – involve the usage of shallowfakes. Creators of influence campaigns continue to depend on conventional film and image editing to influence perceptions online (Brandom, 2019).

Shallowfakes are manipulated images, texts and videos that do not use deep learning algorithms. As a result, shallowfakes do not require the intense skill set and learning required by deep fakes. Shallowfakes are more commonly seen within the information environment and provide a more basic method of influencing opinions. Due to the technical expertise and large amount of data to generate a deepfake using deep learning algorithms, shallowfakes remain a simpler and more cost-effective tool.

Edited videos and photos in shallowfakes involve little to no technology tools to create. They are often mis-contextualized and can range from crudely altered videos to sleekly manipulated images (Schick, 2020). The manipulation of shallowfakes using non-AI tools include the deliberate slowing down or speeding up of a video to reframe the actual meaning of the video to mislead viewers. The splicing together of different video clips of a speech can drastically change the original intention of the video – changing start and end points of the video can diminish or remove context needed to understand the intention of the original video (Leetaru, 2019). For instance, a shallowfake of US House Speaker Nancy Pelosi was manipulated by slowing down the original footage to give the effect of drunkenness and slowness of speech and behavior, seeking to discredit her reputation (Reuters, 2020).

Misinformation from shallowfakes has led to violence. In India, rumors of alleged child abduction in rural villages resulted in a spate of mob lynching and deaths. Mis-contextualized viral videos disseminated on WhatsApp spurred vigilante mobs to attack suspected individuals of alleged kidnappings. (Lahariya, 2019). Text and image-based misinformation spread on platforms such as WhatsApp and Facebook could be further amplified by convincing deep fakes.

Research has noted that combinations of shallowfakes and inauthentic coordinated behavior using automated social media accounts (bots) networks to encourage virality and dissemination on social media and messaging platforms are prevalent among influence operations globally (Bradshaw & Howard, 2019).Influence operation activities in Asia have been observed in countries including Myanmar, the Philippines, Indonesia and Malaysia, such as the usage of cyber troops to run networks of fake accounts to share content (including shallowfakes) with various political narratives.

Shallowfakes, while crude and doctored with simple editing tools, are undoubtedly impactful and should not be underestimated, especially when false information is weaponized to spread animosity along ethnic, racial and religious lines (Sample, 2020). Shallowfakes amplify existing tensions and fault lines, making it prime for abuse and weaponization for covert and malicious purposes to disseminate disinformation – misconstruing original intent to prey upon fears and biases. The level of sophistication and believability involved in shallowfake creation and dissemination online does not have to be at the same technological level as deep fakes for shallowfakes to be effective and damaging (Sonnemaker, 2021).

Existing lower-level technological versions of disinformation has led to violence and conflict in Myanmar. The viral dissemination of shallowfakes on social media has fueled large-scale violence of the minority ethnic Rohingya Muslims in 2018 (Mozur, 2018). Despite improvements to moderation policies and the removal of inauthentic coordinated behavior by social media platforms (Facebook, 2020a), shallowfakes are still pervasive, with outflows of Rohingya refugees and sustained communal violence recurring. Shallowfakes on social media have been used for hate speech and disinformation purposes in part due to the Tatmadaw condoning radical voices against the Rohingyas online for political purposes (Sinpeng & Tapsell, 2020). In 2021, Burmese of Chinese descent have been targeted by disinformation and misinformation alike, over a range of perceived grievances (e.g., questioning the loyalty or the allegiance to the Burmese people) and rumors (e.g., allegations of Chinese engineers helping the military to shut down the internet), and triggered a spate of violence against Chinese Burmese and businesses (Nagao & Shima, 2021).

The deployment of shallowfakes in Indonesia has also stoked sectarian tensions. The country has grappled with covert disinformation online campaigns in the country (Allard & Stubbs, 2020). An edited video of former Jakarta governor Basuki Tjahaja Purnama went viral on Facebook in 2016, leading to his conviction of blasphemy in 2017 (Coconuts Jakarta, 2016). In the original video, Basuki remarked that his electoral opponents misquoted Quranic verses to support their political agenda. The video was edited with poorly captioned subtitles and uploaded to messaging and social media platforms, with a key component of Basuki's speech edited out of the video, creating the perception that his remarks targeted the Islamic holy book, the Quran, instead of his opponents. This resulted in outrage in the predominantly Muslim majority nation and led to massive protests for and against the politician.[3] Another instance involved the dissemination of edited video clips featuring Rizieq Shihab, the controversial leader of the now-banned Islam Defenders Front (FPI). Supporters of Shihab had claimed that the clips were deep fakes used to manipulate the audio and visual content of the video (Yang Hui, 2020).

The act of labeling a shallowfake video as a deepfake, while disputed, has the potential to undermine public trust in traditional sources of authority such as the media and news agencies (Minsky, 2021). These tactics are similar when allegations of authentic videos are dubbed as deep fakes. Poorly edited shallowfakes have been accused as being deep fakes, and vice versa, for purposes of discrediting authority and institutions. A recent example in Myanmar involving a video on state-run media allegedly showed the former Chief Minister of Yangon confessing to bribing ousted leader Aung San Suu Kyi with gold bars. The poorly edited video – containing voices and lip movements which were out of sync and distorted – led netizens online to label the video a deepfake and part of a campaign to discredit Aung San Suu Kyi and the anti-junta movement. Experts, however, reported that the video was not a deepfake, but a crude shallowfake (Devanesan, 2021). This seeks to illustrate the ambiguity and confusion of whether poorly shot or edited videos are considered a cheapfake or a deepfake. Furthermore, results can be disputed despite technical analysis conducted to demonstrate if a video is a shallowfake or a deepfake, due to the reinforcement of individual biases and beliefs. Shallowfakes can be convincing to individuals and can alter opinions even after they are debunked (Minsky, 2021).

Both deep fakes and shallowfakes contribute toward the damage of public trust, which works in favor of disinformation actors. People in Asia are concerned (WITNESS, 2020) that the most immediate threat posed by the weaponization of synthetic media for malicious purposes would be the diminished trust in which it would engender, where the deployment of such synthetic media could threaten democratic processes of elections and journalism. For instance, deep fakes that hijack credible media brands or agencies could erode the trust in which journalism functions. Furthermore, the cases of nonconsensual deep fakes could also result in greater cyberbullying or blackmailing efforts to damage reputations and careers.

## Existing Measures for Tackling Deep fakes

### *Legislation*

While there have been global legislative efforts in tackling the issue of deep fakes, most deepfake laws are geared toward politics and more specifically revolve around election interference and foreign influence using disinformation tactics.

The United States' National Defense Authorization Act 2020 (NDAA) contains provisions relating to machine-manipulated media and requires the Director of National Intelligence to submit unclassified reports to the US Congress on the foreign weaponization of deep fakes. The NDAA 2021 has been expanded to study the broad range of dangers posed by such false media, for example, the usage of deep fakes for fraud or the violation of civil rights laws, and nonconsensual deepfake pornography (Ferraro, 2020). Various states in the United States have written to address deep fakes. California, for instance, "makes it illegal for anyone to intentionally distribute deep fakes intended to deceive voters or harm a candidate's reputation within 60 days of an election" (Castro, 2020). Similar legislative efforts are also underway in the United Kingdom. While the United Kingdom currently has no laws specifically targeting deep fakes, the UK Law commission reviewing deepfake images and videos will aim to provide proposals for legislation (Elks, 2021).

In Singapore, the Protection from Online Falsehoods and Manipulation Act (POFMA) was enacted in 2019 to tackle deliberate online falsehoods, including deep fakes. This was done after a select parliamentary committee was formed to study the problem of deliberate online falsehoods. The Committee noted the dangers of deep fakes as they can be "created relatively easily and cheaply" (Parliament of Singapore, 2018). Similar legislation is also in place in Vietnam (Nguyen & Pearson, 2020) and Cambodia (New Straits Times, 2020).

China has also clamped down on deep fakes. The Cyberspace Administration of China (CAC) has pushed forward with legislation in 2020, banning publishing of deep fakes without proper disclosure of the usage of AI or virtual reality technology. The CAC stated that deepfake technology could "endanger national security, disrupt social stability, disrupt social order and infringe upon the legitimate rights and interests of others" (Reuters, 2019a). Failure to provide proper disclosure is considered a criminal offence. The CAC has also further legislative provisions to tackle deep fakes, with technology applications such as deep learning must not be utilized for the engagement of activities prohibited by laws (Chen, 2020).

### Education and Community

The creation of deep fakes for educational purposes to raise awareness of its potential has garnered much attention and engagement. During the 2020 US presidential election campaign, RepresentUs, a US NGO, developed deepfake videos of North Korean president Kim Jong Un and Russian President Vladimir Putin, as part of an advertisement campaign to highlight the importance of protecting voting rights. In the videos, the deepfaked leaders mentioned how the democracy of the United States could be undermined from within the country. The campaign's goal was to prompt voters to check their voting registration ballots.[4] The videos, originally intended to be aired on television during the presidential debates in the United States, were ultimately pulled by major television networks but were shared on social media platforms – with most people commenting that these videos were uncanny and helped educate about the dangers of deep fakes and disinformation (Kahn, 2020).

The *explicit* mention or disclosure of a deepfake video to the audience can be effective in gaining attention. Some educational efforts utilizing deep fakes, while good-intentioned, can unfortunately backfire. A 2018 video of then US President Donald Trump calling on Belgium to withdraw from the Paris climate agreement, released by the Flemish Socialist political party, resulted in anger over the usage of the deepfake (von der Burchard, 2018).[5] Though the intention of the video was to encourage citizens to sign a petition urging the Belgian government for urgent action on climate change, the campaign creators had overestimated the ability of audiences in discerning the inauthenticity of the video.[6] This reinforces the notion that individuals misjudge the artificiality and authenticity of a video or image and accuracy in their ability to determine deepfake.

The journalistic community in various Asian countries contributes toward reinforcement of education efforts on the issue of disinformation, misinformation and deep fakes. Nongovernmental organizations in Asia have played a prominent role in media literacy efforts. MAFINDO, an Indonesian NGO fact-checking entity (which started from a grassroot organization) and a member of the International Fact Checking Network, is part of a digital verification collective in the country called Cek Fakta ("to fact-check"), with Indonesian major news outlets such as Detik and Tempo as media partners. Together, the collective refutes and addresses false information (Facebook, 2019). Existing media literacy and fact-checking initiatives can continue to play a role in raising public awareness against deep fakes.

### *Technology*

Efforts by technology and social media companies to tackle deep fakes have taken on greater prominence since the 2020 US presidential election. Facebook, for instance, announced in January 2020 that it would remove deep fakes from its platform.[7] It has also developed technical tools for deepfake detection to reveal the origins of uploaded deep fakes and identify the design of the AI model used (Shead, 2021). TikTok, in response to the highly realistic Tom Cruise content on the platform, has said that it will not act against Chris Ume's @deeptomcruise account as it did not violate policies against harmful deep fakes (TikTok, 2020). In Asia, leading online platforms in China have implemented algorithmic detection techniques to ensure internal compliance to remove harmful content, including deep fakes which aim to mislead or deceive. For instance, Tencent has developed a product called Anti-Deepfake for businesses operating on its platform via Tencent Cloud (Tencent, n.d.).

Tech companies are not the only ones developing policies or products to tackle deep fakes. In Asia, technological innovations have been developed. For instance, Singapore's national identity scheme utilizes facial biometrics to not only detect the identity of a citizen but also to detect whether a person is genuinely present – that is, not a deepfake (McDonald, 2020). AI Singapore, a national artificial intelligence (AI) program, has also recently launched Trusted Media Challenge, an international competition to combat deep fakes, collaborating with news agencies in Singapore to provide a database of 800 videos (Kurohi, 2021). The Korea Advanced Institute of Science and Technology (KAIST) unveiled a deepfake detection mobile app KaiCatch, which calculates the likelihood of an uploaded image being manipulated (Yonhap News Agency, 2021). In India, Fake-Buster, a deepfake detector, was developed to identify manipulated media on social media platforms (Dharmaraj, 2021). Apps such as Reface limit deepfake creation to ten-second videos or GIFs and are expanding digital watermarking to their users (Smith, 2020). Start-ups focusing on deep fakes as a core area of business are choosing to deploy the technology narrowly to avoid potential abuse. For instance, Kapwing, a start-up which makes video editing tools for influencers, limited its deepfake tools for its users (Hao, 2020).

Deepfake detection technology, however, has its limitations. Research has shown that even deepfake detectors can be tricked into misidentifying a deepfake video (Mirsky & Lee, 2021). The Tom Cruise deepfake videos created by Chris Ume, for instance, were able to fool detection software into thinking that the fake videos were authentic (Stern, 2021).[8] While experts in digital video forensics agree that the videos were by far the most realistic and high quality they had seen, human video forensic analysts manually examined the videos and were able to spot tell-tale signs of inauthenticity (Kahn, 2021a). Technical methods for catching deep fakes have also thus far been unsuccessful in catching shallowfakes such as the altered video of Nancy Pelosi (Hao, 2019).

## Potential Prescriptions

Though synthetic media promises to provide ways to effectively replicate day-to-day reality, there are risks despite legitimate commercial uses for synthetic media. As elaborated in the previous sections, synthetic media, however, can be weaponized for the deployment of deep fakes and disinformation purposes. A few points on potential prescriptions are laid out in this section to elaborate on the possible ways forward.

### *A Taxonomy on What Constitutes a Deepfake*

Experts have suggested a reframing of the term "deepfake" (Schick, 2020). The deepfake label has been synonymous with misinformation and tainted with negativity with malicious use but is also commonly used to describe synthetic media for legitimate, commercial content. The term "deepfake" has been misunderstood by the public as media stories are used to highlight the dangers of deep fakes, with an emphasis on the growing sophistication of deepfake technology (Vincent, 2018). The overuse of the term could cast doubts on the authenticity and credibility of legitimate content. Such doubt can be misused to sow uncertainty and confusion among the public, undermining the evaluation of truthful and factual content in an already uncertain and cloudy information environment. Experts such as Nina Schick have sought to define a deepfake as any synthetic media used solely for the purposes of disinformation and misinformation (Schick, 2020). A nuanced explanation of what constitutes a deepfake, and its current deepfake technology capabilities, can provide a greater public understanding of its current capabilities and contribute to general discourse and public attitudes toward synthetic media writ large.

### More Diverse Voices from Other Parts of the World, Including Asia

Conversations about deep fakes have occurred mostly in the United States and Europe, where solutions to tackling deep fakes are being rapidly developed. Voices from Asia are much-needed as the ramifications of deep fakes and shallowfakes would be greatly felt in the region. Greater prominence can be given to media literacy initiatives stemming from Asia, and best practices and strategies within the region can be spotlighted and shared globally. Platforms such as WITNESS can be a great start to facilitate such initiatives. Asian voices can also contribute toward a general taxonomy on deep fakes, as mentioned earlier.

### Emphasize Visual Literacy as Part of Media Literacy Toolbox

The awareness and understanding of deep fakes in Asia are rather scant. Public engagement with deep fakes should continue as it can help inoculate people to the potential harms of deep fakes and the emerging advancements of deepfake AI technology. Individuals who are unaware of the technology could be the most vulnerable to fall for it.

Research by Ahmed (2020) found that in Singapore, one in two Singaporeans are unaware of deep fakes, and that one in three Singaporeans had inadvertently shared deep fakes online. Furthermore, due to the cognitive bias of "third-person perception," individuals overemphasize their ability to recognize and be more resilient to false information than others.[9]

This presents a gap in media literacy efforts – specifically in visual literacy, where people might overestimate or think that it is relatively simple to distinguish between authentic and inauthentic visual content and might overlook subtle differences in distinguishing between the two (Gault, 2021). Research by Newman et al. (2015) revealed that people are comparatively weak in guarding against visual deception. Existing media literacy and fact-checking initiatives can continue to play a role in raising public awareness against shallowfakes and deep fakes while raising the importance of visual literacy.

Educational content can create engagement for visual literacy awareness. "Which Face Is Real," for instance, utilizes images generated by thispersondoesnotexist.com to test individuals on their ability to distinguish real from AI-generated faces. Initiatives could be also established to enhance visual literacy through the incorporation of multidisciplinary research. The Visual Understanding Initiative at Sydney University, for instance, aims to explore the neurological basis of visual understanding and its applicability in training to spot fakes (Power, 2021). Such an initiative could be launched in Asia as well.

However, caution is needed, as an over-inflationary concern over deep fakes may amplify the decision to disengage from applying critical thinking analysis and seek out information sources which lean favorably toward preexisting views (Harwell, 2019).

### Empowering Capacity-Building for Journalists

Journalists are concerned that the impact of deep fakes would erode the trust in which media functions. Investigative tactics adopted by fact-checkers and journalists continue to be held in good stead when verifying deep fakes. In addition to deepfake detection software, techniques such as Google reverse image search and internet searches online are more robust compared to advances in deepfake technology (Hao, 2021). However, a lack of deepfake detection capacity and tools to counter deep fakes is also among the concerns of news media (WITNESS, 2020). The importance of placing detection tools into the hands of journalists has never been more important, as journalists are often the first line of defense against the spread of misinformation (Sohrawardi & Wright, 2020).

Journalists, however, currently do not have good ways to verify deepfake videos (Funke, 2018). Limitations in detection technology hinder journalists from deepfake verification, and technological capabilities are still exclusive to academics and companies. More collaboration between the media, civil society, fact-checkers, academia and technology companies can ensure greater preparedness. One suggestion mooted by journalists involves a database of experts that can be a source of reference for fact-checkers locally, regionally and globally. This can be built upon existing fact-checking initiatives within a country. For instance, the Indonesian digital verification collective Cek Fakta has played a prominent role in refuting and addressing false information but is limited by a lack of technical tools, especially for detecting deep fakes (WITNESS, 2020).

The ability to verify audiovisual content is increasingly important for journalists, and having adequate resources and technical capabilities to do so contributes toward the success of fact-checking. NGOs such as WITNESS have conducted workshops on deep fakes in Asia, Latin America and the United States to raise awareness on the challenges deep fakes bring to the industry. The International Fact-Checking Network (IFCN), a unit of the Poynter Institute, can incorporate tools and resources to share among fact-checkers and journalists globally.

## Conclusion

Technological advances will bring about innovation in synthetic media for industries worldwide. This would bring about greater opportunities for the weaponization of synthetic media for deep fakes, be it for cybercrime or for the political manipulation and influence of audiences globally. The systemic impact with the proliferation of falsehoods is not that they are believed, as explained by Arendt (1978), but rather that cynicism pervades, which then emboldens the incumbent and status quo. The risk of underestimating the impact of deep fakes could be potentially dangerous as governments and societies cope with the challenges posed by disinformation.

## Acknowledgment

The author would like to express her gratitude to Benjamin Ang, Senior Fellow and Deputy Head of the Centre of Excellence for National Security (CENS) at the S. Rajaratnam School of International Studies (RSIS), Nanyang Technological University (NTU), for providing feedback on an earlier draft of this manuscript.

## Notes

1   Disinformation is classified as the malicious intent to deceive. It can be defined as the "false information deliberately and often covertly spread in order to influence public opinion or obscure the truth." Misinformation, on the other hand, can be defined as "incorrect or misleading information," regardless of intent to deceive. See *Merriam-Webster*, *Disinformation*, www.merriam-webster. com/dictionary/disinformation; *Merriam-Webster*, *Misinformation*, www. merriam-webster.com/dictionary/misinformation. Also see M. Gebel (2021). Misinformation vs. Disinformation: What to Know about Each form of False Information, and How to Spot Them Online. *Business Insider*. www.business insider.com/misinformation-vs-disinformation

2   The video went viral with no indication or labeling that it was a deepfake.

3   The editor and uploader of the viral video ultimately was sentenced to jail for spreading hate speech in 2017.

4   The videos carried the tagline "This footage isn't real, but the threat to democracy is."

5   The "Trump" in the video mentioned that the video is fake: "We all know climate change is fake, just like this video." However, this was overlooked by most viewers. See J. Vincent (2018). Why We Need a Better Definition of "Deepfake." *The Verge*. www.theverge.com/2018/5/22/17380306/deepfake-definition-ai-manipulation-fake-news.

6   It later turned out that the video was created using Adobe After Effects. See D. Funke (2018). A Potential New Marketing Strategy for Political Campaigns: Deepfake Videos. *Poynter*. www.poynter.org/fact-checking/2018/a-potential-new-marketing-strategy-for-political-campaigns-deepfake-videos/.

7   Facebook announced it would remove misleading manipulated videos if they had been edited in ways which "aren't apparent to an average person and would likely mislead someone" and includes "product of artificial intelligence or machine learning . . . making it appear to be authentic." See Facebook (2020).

*Enforcing Against Manipulated Media.* https://about.fb.com/news/2020/01/enforcing-against-manipulated-media/.

8   Ume utilized powerful graphics processing computer hardware, a massive database of Tom Cruise images (13,000 initial images, and a smaller dataset containing an additional 5,000 to 6,000 images) and manually editing the videos using conventional computer video-editing software, combining deep fakes with conventional computer-generated imagery (CGI) and visual effects (VFX). The whole process took a total of two months to complete. See J. Kahn (2021). Deepfake Master Behind Those Viral Tom Cruise Videos Says the Technology Should be Regulated. *Fortune.* https://fortune.com/2021/03/05/tom-cruise-deepfake-creator-technology-should-be-regulated/.

9   A survey by Ipsos Singapore revealed that while eight in ten Singaporeans surveyed were confident in their ability to identify "fake news," 45% had incorrectly identified fake news stories. The survey revealed that the levels of vulnerability to fake news were higher among those aged 15–24. See Ipsos (2018). *The Susceptibility of Singaporeans Towards Fake News.* www.ipsos.com/en-sg/susceptibility-singaporeans-towards-fake-news.

# References

Adee, S. (2020, April 29). What are Deepfakes and How are They Created? *IEEE Spectrum.* https://spectrum.ieee.org/tech-talk/computing/software/what-are-deepfakes-how-are-they-created

Adjer, H., Patrini, G., Cavalli, F., & Cullen, L. (2019). *The State of Deepfakes: Landscape, Threats and Impact.* Deeptrace Labs.

Agarwal, S., Farid, H., Gu, Y., He, M., Nagano, K., & Hao, L. (2019). *Protecting World Leaders against Deep Fakes.* CVPR Workshops, pp. 38–45. https://openaccess.thecvf.com/content_CVPRW_2019/papers/Media%20Forensics/Agarwal_Protecting_World_Leaders_Against_Deep_Fakes_CVPRW_2019_paper.pdf?source=post_page

Ahmed, S. (2021). Who Inadvertently Shares Deepfakes? Analyzing the Role of Political Interest, Cognitive Ability, and Social Network Size. *Telematics and Informatics,* 57. https://doi.org/10.1016/j.tele.2020.101508

Allard, T., & Stubbs, J. (2020, January 8). Indonesian Army Wields Internet 'News' as a Weapon in Papua. *Reuters.* www.reuters.com/article/us-indonesia-military-websites-insight-idUSKBN1Z7001

Arendt, H. (1978, October 26). Hannah Arendt: From an Interview. *The New York Review of Books.* www.nybooks.com/articles/1978/10/26/hannah-arendt-from-an-interview/

Ayyub, R. (2018, November 21). I was the Victim of a Deepfake Porn Plot Intended to Silence Me. *Huffington Post.* www.huffingtonpost.co.uk/entry/deepfake-porn_uk_5bf2c126e4b0f32bd58ba316

BBC. (2019, June 13). *Deepfake Videos Could 'Spark' Violent Social Unrest.* www.bbc.com/news/technology-48621452

Boo, S. (2019, June 17). Report: Experts Say Sex Videos not Fake, But Can't Confirm Azmin's Identity. *Yahoo News.* https://sg.news.yahoo.com/report-experts-sex-videos-not-094410155.html

Bradshaw, S., & Howard, P. (2019). The Global Disinformation Order: 2019 Global Inventory of Organised Social Media Manipulation. *The Computational Propaganda Research Project.* https://comprop.oii.ox.ac.uk/wp-content/uploads/sites/93/2019/09/CyberTroop-Report19.pdf

Brandom, R. (2019, March 5). Deepfake Propaganda is not a Real Problem. *The Verge.* www.theverge.com/2019/3/5/18251736/deepfake-propaganda-misinformation-troll-video-hoax

Breland, A. (2019, March 15). The Bizarre and Terrifying Case of the "Deepfake" Video that Helped Bring an African Nation to the Brink. *Mother Jones.* www.motherjones.com/politics/2019/03/deepfake-gabon-ali-bongo/

Burgess, M. (2020, August 27). Deepfake Porn is Now Mainstream. And Major Sites are Cashing in. *WIRED.* www.wired.co.uk/article/deepfake-porn-websites-videos-law

Castro, D. (2020). Deepfakes are on the Rise – How Should Government Respond? *Government Technology.* www.govtech.com/policy/Deepfakes-Are-on-the-Rise-How-Should-Government-Respond.html

Chen, J. (2020, September 15). Deepfakes. *Asia Society.* https://asiasociety.org/sites/default/files/inline-files/Final%20Deepfake%20PDF.pdf

Chesney, R., & Citron, D. K. (2018). Deep Fakes: A Looming Challenge for Privacy, Democracy and National Security. 107 California Law Review 1753 (2019), U of Texas Law, Public Law Research Paper No. 692, U of Maryland Legal Studies Research Paper No. 2018–21. http://dx.doi.org/10.2139/ssrn.3213954

Chesney, R., Citron, D. K., & Farid, H. (2020, May 11). All's Clear for Deepfakes: Think Again. *Lawfare.* www.lawfareblog.com/alls-clear-deepfakes-think-again

Christopher, N. (2020, February 18). We've Just Seen the First Use of Deepfakes in an Indian Election Campaign. *VICE.* www.vice.com/en/article/jgedjb/the-first-use-of-deepfakes-in-indian-election-by-bjp

CNN. (2021, March 2). *No, Tom Cruise isn't on TikTok. It's a Deepfake.* https://edition.cnn.com/videos/business/2021/03/02/tom-cruise-tiktok-deepfake-orig.cnn-business/video/playlists/stories-worth-watching/

Coconuts Jakarta. (2016, November 8). *Netizens Debate the Use of the Word #pakai to Determine Whether or not Ahok Insulted the Quran.* https://coconuts.co/jakarta/news/netizens-debate-use-word-pakai-determine-whether-or-not-ahok-insulted-quran/

Cole, S. (2018, January 25). We are Truly Fucked: Everyone is Making AI-Generated Fake Porn Now. *VICE.* www.vice.com/en/article/bjye8a/reddit-fake-porn-app-daisy-ridley

Cole, S. (2019, June 27). This Horrifying App Undresses a Photo of Any Woman with a Single Click. *VICE.* www.vice.com/en/article/kzm59x/deepnude-app-creates-fake-nudes-of-any-woman

Corera, G. (2021, April 20). MI5 Warns of Spies Using LinkedIn to Trick Staff into Spilling Secrets. *BBC.* www.bbc.com/news/technology-56812746

Devanesan, J. (2021, April 1). Info Cyberwars – The Dark Side of Tech in the Myanmar Coup. *Techwire Asia.* https://techwireasia.com/2021/04/info-cyberwars-the-dark-side-of-tech-in-the-myanmar-coup/

Dharmaraj, S. (2021, May 22). Indian Researchers Develop Deepfake Detection Technology. *OpenGov*. https://opengovasia.com/indian-researchers-develop-deepfake-detection-technology/

Diakopoulos, N., & Johnson, D. (2020). Anticipating and Addressing the Ethical Implications of Deepfakes in the Context of Elections. *New Media & Society*. https://doi.org/10.1177/1461444820925811

Elks, S. (2021, February 26). Sharing 'Deepfake' Porn Images should be a Crime, Says British Law Body. *Reuters*. www.reuters.com/article/britain-women-lawmaking-idUKL8N2KU7NL

Facebook. (2019, June 12). *How Mafindo Went from a Grassroots Movement to a National Fact-Checking Outlet*. www.facebook.com/journalismproject/mafindo-facebook-third-party-fact-checking

Facebook. (2020a, October 27). *Removing Coordinated Inauthentic Behaviour*. https://about.fb.com/news/2020/10/removing-coordinated-inauthentic-behavior-mexico-iran-myanmar/

Facebook. (2020b, September 22). *Removing Coordinated Inauthentic Behaviour*. https://about.fb.com/news/2020/09/removing-coordinated-inauthentic-behavior-china-philippines/

Facebook. (2021). *Threat Report: The State of Influence Operations 2017–2020*. https://about.fb.com/wp-content/uploads/2021/05/IO-Threat-Report-May-20-2021.pdf

Federal Bureau of Investigation. (2021, March 10). *Malicious Actors Almost Certainly Will Leverage Synthetic Content for Cyber and Foreign Influence Operations*. www.ic3.gov/Media/News/2021/210310-2.pdf

Ferraro, M. (2020, December 29). Congress's Deepening Interest in Deepfakes. *The Hill*. https://thehill.com/opinion/cybersecurity/531911-congresss-deepening-interest-in-deepfakes

Funke, D. (2018, May 4). 10 Tips for Verifying Viral Social Media Videos. *Poynter*. www.poynter.org/fact-checking/2018/10-tips-for-verifying-viral-social-media-videos/

Gault, M. (2021, March 26). Think You Can Tell the Difference Between Human and AI? Take This Test. *VICE*. www.vice.com/en/article/pkdj8g/think-you-can-tell-the-difference-between-human-and-ai-take-this-test?mc_cid=10cbf789d9&mc_eid=3041e908df

Graphika. (2021). *Fake Cluster Boosts Huawei: Accounts with GAN Faces Attack Belgium Over 5G Restrictions*. https://public-assets.graphika.com/reports/graphika_report_fake_cluster_boosts_huawei.pdf

GRC World Forums. (2021, June 2). *GRCTV – Episode 2 – AI & Synthetic Media*. www.grcworldforums.com/grc-tv/grctv-episode-2-ai-and-synthetic-media/1901.article

Hao, K. (2019, October 19). The Biggest Threat of Deepfakes isn't the Deepfakes Themselves. *MIT Technology Review*. www.technologyreview.com/2019/10/10/132667/the-biggest-threat-of-deepfakes-isnt-the-deepfakes-themselves/

Hao, K. (2020, August 28). Memes are Making Deepfakes, and Things are Getting Weird. *MIT Technology Review*. www.technologyreview.com/2020/08/28/1007746/ai-deepfakes-memes/

Hao, K. (2021, March 31). Deepfake "Amazon Workers" are Sowing Confusion on Twitter. That's not the Problem. *MIT Technology Review*. www.technologyreview.com/2021/03/31/1021487/deepfake-amazon-workers-are-sowing-confusion-on-twitter-thats-not-the-problem/

Harwell, D. (2019, June 12). Top AI Researchers Race to Detect 'Deepfake' Videos: 'We are Outgunned'. *The Washington Post*. www.washingtonpost.com/technology/2019/06/12/top-ai-researchers-race-detect-deepfake-videos-we-are-outgunned/

Harwell, D. (2020, October 20). A Shadowy AI Service has Transformed Thousands of Women's Photos into Fake Nudes: 'Make Fantasy a Reality'. *The Washington Post*. www.washingtonpost.com/technology/2020/10/20/deep-fake-nudes/

Kahn, J. (2020, October 3). These Deepfake Videos of Putin and Kim Have Gone Viral. *Fortune*. https://fortune.com/2020/10/02/deepfakes-putin-kim-jong-un-democracy-disinformation/

Kahn, J. (2021a, March 5). Deepfake Master Behind Those Viral Tom Cruise Videos Says the Technology Should Be Regulated. *Fortune*. https://fortune.com/2021/03/05/tom-cruise-deepfake-creator-technology-should-be-regulated/

Kahn, J. (2021b, March 1). Why Deepfake Creators Love Tom Cruise. *Fortune*. https://fortune.com/2021/03/01/why-deepfake-creators-love-tom-cruise/

Kemp, S. (2020, January 30). Digital 2020: 3.8 Billion People Use Social Media. *We Are Social*. https://wearesocial.com/blog/2020/01/digital-2020-3-8-billion-people-use-social-media

Kurohi, R. (2021, July 15). AI Singapore Launches $700k Competition to Combat Deepfakes. *The Straits Times*. www.straitstimes.com/tech/ai-singapore-launches-700k-competition-to-combat-deepfakes

Lahariya, K. (2019, September 17). "They Pluck Out Hearts of Children" – How Fake News is Crippling Indian Villages with Anxiety. *Quartz*. https://qz.com/india/1710209/rural-india-in-turmoil-over-whatsapp-kidnapping-fake-news/

Leetaru, K. (2019, August 26). The Real Danger Today is Shallow Fakes and Selective Editing not Deep Fakes. *Forbes*. www.forbes.com/sites/kalevleetaru/2019/08/26/the-real-danger-today-is-shallow-fakes-and-selective-editing-not-deep-fakes/?sh=2b2c3df04ea0

Mackintosh, E., & Gupta, S. (2020, January 22). Troll Armies, 'Deepfake' Porn Videos and Violent Threats. How Twitter became so Toxic for India's Women Politicians. *CNN*. https://edition.cnn.com/2020/01/22/india/india-women-politicians-trolling-amnesty-asequals-intl/index.html

McDonald, T. (2020, September 25). Singapore in World First for Facial Verification. *BBC*. www.bbc.com/news/business-54266602

Mengle, G. (2020, April 13). Law Enforcers Worried as Deep Nude Makes a Return. *The Hindu*. www.thehindu.com/news/national/law-enforcers-worried-as-deep-nude-makes-a-return/article31334415.ece

Minsky, C. (2021, January 25). 'Deepfake' Videos: To Believe or not Believe? *The Financial Times*. www.ft.com/content/803767b7-2076-41e2-a587-1f13c77d1675

Mirsky, Y., & Lee, W. (2021). The Creation and Detection of Deepfakes: A Survey. *ACM Computing Surveys*, 54(1), 1–41. https://doi.org/10.1145/3425780

Mozur, P. (2018, October 15). A Genocide Incited on Facebook, with Posts from Myanmar's Military. *The New York Times*. www.nytimes.com/2018/10/15/technology/myanmar-facebook-genocide.html

Nagao, R., & Shima, T. (2021, May 26). From Myanmar to US, Disinformation Floods Social Media. *Nikkei Asia*. https://asia.nikkei.com/Spotlight/Century-of-Data/From-Myanmar-to-US-disinformation-floods-social-media

Newman, E. J., Garry, M., Unkelbach, C., Bernstein, D. M., Lindsay, D., & Nash, R. A. (2015). Truthiness and Falseness of Trivia Claims Depend on Judgmental Contexts. *Journal of Experimental Psychology: Learning, Memory, and Cognition*, 41(5), 1337–1348.

New Straits Times. (2020, December 11). *Cambodia Warns Media Outlets Against Publishing Fake News*. www.nst.com.my/world/region/2020/12/648627/cambodia-warns-media-outlets-against-publishing-fake-news

Nguyen, P., & Pearson, J. (2020, April 15). Vietnam Introduces 'Fake News' Fines for Coronavirus Misinformation. *Reuters*. www.reuters.com/article/us-health-coronavirus-vietnam-security/vietnam-introduces-fake-news-fines-for-coronavirus-misinformation-idUSKCN21X0EB

Nimmo, B., Eid, C. S., & Ronzaud, L. (2020). Operation Naval Gazing: Facebook Takes Down Inauthentic Chinese Network. *Graphika*. https://public-assets.graphika.com/reports/graphika_report_naval_gazing.pdf

Nimmo, B., Eib, C. S., Tamora, L., Johnson, K., Smith, I., Buziashvili, E., Kann, A., Karan, K., de León Rosas, E., & Rizzuto, M. (2019). #OperationFFS: Fake Face Swarm. *Graphika*. https://public-assets.graphika.com/reports/graphika_report_operation_ffs_fake_face_storm.pdf

Parliament of Singapore. (2018). *Report of the Select Committee on Deliberate Online Falsehoods Executive Summary*. www.parliament.gov.sg/docs/default-source/Press-Releases/executive-summary – report-of-the-select-committee-on-deliberate-online-falsehoods.pdf

Power, J. (2021, July 17). From Deepfake Tom Cruise to Sham QR Codes: Can People be Trained to Spot the Hoaxes? *The Sydney Morning Herald*. www.smh.com.au/national/nsw/from-deepfake-tom-cruise-to-sham-qr-codes-can-people-be-trained-to-spot-the-hoaxes-20210714-p589qy.html

Rawnsley, A. (2020, July 7). Right-Wing Media Outlets Duped by a Middle East Propaganda Campaign. *The Daily Beast*. www.thedailybeast.com/right-wing-media-outlets-duped-by-a-middle-east-propaganda-campaign

Reuters. (2019a, November 29). *China Seeks to Root Out Fake News and Deepfakes with New Online Content Rules*. www.reuters.com/article/us-china-technology/china-seeks-to-root-out-fake-news-and-deepfakes-with-new-online-content-rules-idUSKBN1Y30VU

Reuters. (2019b, April 10). *David Beckham's 'Deep Fake' Malaria Awareness Video*. https://mobile.reuters.com/video/watch/david-beckhams-deep-fake-malaria-awarene-id536254167?chan=c1tal5kh

Reuters. (2019c, July 18). *Malaysian Police Say Political Leader Behind Gay Sex Tape Allegations*. www.reuters.com/article/uk-malaysia-politics-idUKKCN1UD0OH

Reuters. (2020, August 4). *Fact Check: "Drunk" Nancy Pelosi Video is Manipulated*. www.reuters.com/article/uk-factcheck-nancypelosi-manipulated-id USKCN24Z2BI

Robertson, A. (2018, February 7). Reddit Bans 'Deepfakes' AI Porn Communities. *The Verge*. www.theverge.com/2018/2/7/16982046/reddit-deepfakes-ai-celebrity-face-swap-porn-community-ban

Rushing, E. (2020, March 9). A Philly Lawyer Nearly Wired $9,000 to a Stranger Impersonating His Son's Voice, Showing Just How Smart Scammers are Getting. *The Philadelphia Inquirer*. www.inquirer.com/news/voice-scam-impersonation-fraud-bail-bond-artificial-intelligence-20200309.html

Ryall, J. (2020, November 20). Celebrity Deepfake Porn Cases in Japan Point to Rise in Sex-Related Cybercrime. *South China Morning Post*. www.scmp.com/week-asia/lifestyle-culture/article/3110748/deepfake-porn-cases-japan-point-rise-sex-related

Ryall, J. (2021, January 22). 'Deepfakes' Rattle South Korea's Tech Culture. DW. https://www.dw.com/en/deepfakes-rattle-south-koreas-tech-culture/a-56310213

Sample, I. (2020, January 13). What are Deepfakes – and How Can You Spot Them? *The Guardian*. www.theguardian.com/technology/2020/jan/13/what-are-deepfakes-and-how-can-you-spot-them

Satter, R. (2019, June 13). Experts: Spy Used AI-Generated Face to Connect with Targets. *AP*. https://apnews.com/article/ap-top-news-artificial-intelligence-social-platforms-think-tanks-politics-bc2f19097a4c4fffaa00de6770b8a60d

Satter, R. (2020, July 15). Deepfake Used to Attack Activist Couples Shows New Disinformation Frontier. *Reuters*. www.reuters.com/article/us-cyber-deepfake-activist-idUSKCN24G15E

Schick, N. (2020). *Deepfakes and the Infocalypse: What You Urgently Need to Know*. Octopus Publishing Group.

Shead, S. (2021, June 16). Facebook Scientists Say They Can Now Tell Where Deepfakes Have Come from. *CNBC*. www.cnbc.com/2021/06/16/facebook-scientists-say-they-can-tell-where-deepfakes-come-from.html

Silverman, C., Lytvynenko, J., & Kung, W. (2020, January 6). Disinformation for Hire: How A New Breed of PR Firms is Selling Lies Online. *BuzzFeed News*. www.buzzfeednews.com/article/craigsilverman/disinformation-for-hire-black-pr-firms

Sinpeng, A., & Tapsell, R. (2020). *From Grassroots Activism to Disinformation: Social Media in Southeast Asia*. ISEAS – Yusof Ishak Institute.

Smith, A. (2020, August 7). Reface: New App Lets You Put Your Face on GIFs – but is It Safe? *The Independent*. www.independent.co.uk/life-style/gadgets-and-tech/news/doublicat-gif-safe-app-deep-fake-celebrities-a9628906.html

Sng, S. (2021, March 18). K-Pop Girl Group Eternity to Debut with Deep-Fake Virtual Idols. *The Straits Times*. www.straitstimes.com/life/entertainment/k-pop-girl-group-eternity-to-debut-with-deep-fake-virtual-idols

Sohrawardi, J., & Wright, M. (2020, October 9). In a Battle of AI versus AI, Researchers are Preparing for the Coming Wave of Deepfake Propaganda. *The*

*Conversation.* https://theconversation.com/in-a-battle-of-ai-versus-ai-researchers-are-preparing-for-the-coming-wave-of-deepfake-propaganda-146536

Solsman, J. (2020, October 22). Deepfake Bot on Telegram is Violating Women by Forging Nudes from Regular Pics. *CNET.* www.cnet.com/news/deepfake-bot-on-telegram-is-violating-women-by-forging-nudes-from-regular-pics/

Sonnemaker, T. (2021, April 2). The Tom Cruise Deepfakes were Hard to Create. But Less Sophisticated 'Shallowfakes' are Already Wreaking Havoc. *Business Insider.* www.businessinsider.com/deepfakes-shallowfakes-cheapfakes-tom-cruise-darpa-medifor-synthetic-media-2021-4

Stern, M. (2021, February 25). Shockingly Real Tom Cruise Deep-fakes are Invading TikTok. *The Daily Beast.* www.thedailybeast.com/shockingly-real-tom-cruise-deepfakes-are-invading-tiktok

Stupp, C. (2019, August 30). Fraudsters Used AI to Mimic CEO's Voice in Unusual Cybercrime Case. *The Wall Street Journal.* www.wsj.com/articles/fraudsters-use-ai-to-mimic-ceos-voice-in-unusual-cybercrime-case-11567157402

Sunstein, C. (2021, January 7). Can the Government Regulate Deepfakes? *The Wall Street Journal.* www.wsj.com/articles/can-the-government-regulate-deepfakes-11610038590

Tencent. (n.d.). 腾讯云换脸甄别 *(Mandarin).* https://cloud.tencent.com/document/product/1203/41951

TikTok. (2020). *Combating Misinformation and Election Interference on TikTok.* https://newsroom.tiktok.com/en-us/combating-misinformation-and-election-interference-on-tiktok

Toews, R. (2020, May 25). Deepfakes are Going to Wreak Havoc on Society. We are not Prepared. *Forbes.* www.forbes.com/sites/robtoews/2020/05/25/deepfakes-are-going-to-wreak-havoc-on-society-we-are-not-prepared/?sh=233edb917494

Vaccari, C., & Chadwick, A. (2020). Deepfakes and Disinformation: Exploring the Impact of Synthetic Political Video on Deception, Uncertainty, and Trust in News. *Social Media + Society,* 6(1). https://doi.org/10.1177/2056305120903408

Venkataramakrishnan, S. (2020, October 12). After Deepfakes, a New Fron-tier of AI Trickery: Fake Faces. *Financial Times.* www.ft.com/content/b50d22ec-db98-4891-86da-af34f06d1cb1

Vincent, J. (2018a). Watch Jordan Peele Use AI to make Barack Obama Deliver a PSA about Fake News. *The Verge.* www.theverge.com/tldr/2018/4/17/17247334/ai-fake-news-video-barack-obama-jordan-peele-buzzfeed

Vincent, J. (2018b). Why We Need a Better Definition of 'Deepfake'. *The Verge.* www.theverge.com/2018/5/22/17380306/deepfake-definition-ai-manipulation-fake-news

Vincent, J. (2019). A Spy Reportedly Used an AI-Generated Profile Picture to Connect with Sources on LinkedIn. *The Verge.* www.theverge.com/2019/6/13/18677341/ai-generated-fake-faces-spy-linked-in-contacts-associated-press

Vincent, J. (2021). Lip-Syncing App Wombo Shows the Messy, Meme-Laden Potential of Deepfakes. *The Verge.* www.theverge.com/2021/3/11/22323271/wombo-ai-memes-deepfake-app-lip-sync

von der Burchard, H. (2018). Belgian Socialist Party Circulates 'Deep Fake' Donald Trump Video. *Politico*. www.politico.eu/article/spa-donald-trump-belgium-paris-climate-agreement-belgian-socialist-party-circulates-deep-fake-trump-video/

WITNESS. (2020). *Deepfakes: Prepare Now – Practical Solutions against the Malicious Uses of AI-Manipulated Media.* https://lab.witness.org/wp-content/uploads/sites/29/2020/09/DeepfakesPrepareNow_SoutheastAsia_2020.pdf

Yang Hui, J. (2020). Preparing to Counter the Challenges of Deepfakes in Indonesia. *The Jakarta Post.* www.thejakartapost.com/paper/2020/12/17/preparing-to-counter-the-challenges-of-deepfakes-in-indonesia.html

Yonhap News Agency. (2021). *KAIST Unveils Deepfake-Detecting Mobile App.* https://en.yna.co.kr/view/AEN20210330004200320

# 3   On the Depth of Fakeness

*Eunsong Kim*

*

*Boxing Helena* is a 1993 film about a surgeon who forcefully amputates a woman and holds her hostage in a clear glass box in his home. Initially billed as a dark comedy, the plot unravels as reality to conclude with a scene of Helena waking up in a hospital, situating the events to be her dream. Attached at first to stars such as Madonna and Kim Basinger, the movie was a box office failure and became a source of liberal feminist criticism, to which the writer/director Jennifer Lynch responded by claiming the work to be one of fairy tale and fantasy.

As one of the crudest depictions of objectification, there are several aspects of the film that are useful in the examination of deep fakes. Though advertised as user-friendly, this emerging technology is understood as requiring some specialized knowledge *with* the will to manipulate preexisting representation. Such as the figure of the surgeon, the film locates the executer of fantasy and torture to be a person of superior knowledge, who wields it to manifest his desires. The doctor's fantasy of being together with Helena comes as the removal of her bodily autonomy, and the mutilation of her body is represented as desire, care and then dream.

I open with a description of a campy film from the 1990s to discuss the cultural architecture behind deepfake technology. *Boxing Helena* serves as one cultural primer of how misogyny becomes mediated as augmentation and normalized as desire, and this violence manifests historically through the technical operations of image making. Because though deep fakes have been sensationalized as a new political and financial threat, the tool/weapon was formed via gendered violence, where the heads and voices of women were surgically removed and attached to the bodies of other women, clarifying how the inventions of new technologies codify within them the operations and politics of the culture from which they were produced.

The first deepfake functioned as celebrity porn, where the faces of famous women were composited onto the bodies of less famous or anonymous

DOI: 10.4324/9781003173397-3

actors and persons – all without the permission of the people within the frame. Thus, the figure of the women – much like Helena – in these fakes functions as a didactic encapsulation of the subject-turned-object. And while the procedure of objecthood is considered narratively despicable, perhaps illiberal, it is also the law. Copyright abides by the entitlements of photographers and not the subjects inside them, and cases surrounding fair use and appropriation prioritize the manipulation of the *original* as a sign of authorship. Historically, US Copyright abides by the entitlements of photographers and not the subjects inside them, and cases surrounding fair use and appropriation prioritize the manipulation of the original as a sign of authorship. As such, legal precedents have afforded almost no property claims or protections to the persons captured inside of the frame. How these laws work as the cultural blueprint for deep fakes will be examined in this chapter.

Importantly, that the nightmare/fantasy is premised as one of Helena's own making is reminiscent of the ways perpetrators of gendered violence revert the blame back onto the subject who has been harmed – for smiling, for sharing, for posing, for sending, for existing as the object of fantasy – the harm is their individuated dream/nightmare. If people didn't share images of their bodies, if actors didn't film such scenes, if they acted differently or more *properly* – if only if. Rather than questioning the repetitive constitution of fantasies that revolve around turning a person into an object, it is rationalized that some can avoid victimhood if they simply acted more [fill in the blank].

As machine learning carries with it the legal quandary of black box enclosure, *Boxing Helena* serves as a clear box into how inventions and new technologies codify within them the operations and politics of the culture from which they were produced.[1] Critics often fixate on the creation of new laws and software to remedy the problems brought forth by deep fakes, a strategy that affirms the very technocratic problems it seeks to fix. Such solutions elide the deep and structural problem at hand. In this chapter I argue against treating deep fakes as an isolated phenomena that can be controlled by new software, other kinds of machine learning programs and better laws, but as rather the embodiment of technology developed through colonial imaginations and the material operations of power in this world. I trace the racialized and gendered logic behind image and image rights in order to examine how digital technologies are held together with the history of image construction, be it the Hollywood-level computer-generated imagery (CGI) to user-generated deep fakes. The history of image making coincides with the development of image manipulation, which spans from early darkroom techniques, to the racialized foundations of lighting, to removing artifacts such as watches and clothing before the shot in order to render Indigenous persons premodern, to CGI and compositing, to the use of AI to blend multiple frames. In this trajectory, the manifestation of patriarchy, capitalism and the racial and colonial dynamics of image making remains foundational to the proliferation of deep fakes.

Additionally, if deep fakes have taught us anything it is that emerging technologies are produced at an accelerated rate that outpaces the procedure of lawmaking. Instead, those of us with concerns for the subject captured by the image frame must demand that old laws be amended or abolished, and examine to transform the culture surrounding image making. Shifting the onus from "fixing" one tech to the entire world is not to remove responsibility or to make the problem impossible; rather, it is for their interconnection to be materialized.

In making my argument I situate three main concerns. First, I reorient the conversation of "real" and "fake" from this digital moment to the analog history of racialized photographic imaging and its prioritization of the colonizer and whiteness. The prioritization of whiteness in early photography leads to the development of analog cameras and light systems invented to aestheticize whiteness and coloniality. This hardware legacy becomes foundational to how post-production and image software becomes built to remedy to foundational problems of what hardware refused to see. This understanding of software leads to the development of CGI and compositing, which becomes foundational to how machine learning is deployed to arrogate neural networking systems to create deep fakes. In the continuum of crises of bettering the quality of fakeness, there is the crisis of the fakeness of the camera, the fakeness of light sensors: all of which has been pivotal to the construction of the ideal, analog and digital human.

Second, I overview how image rights and legal provisions for photographer, artist and creator have come to situate the crisis highlighted by deep fakes. That anyone, but predominately women, have been the targets of this tech demonstrates how the history of photography, colonialism and copyright has positioned the owner of the image as the photographer, recorder of the frame, over the desires and contestations of the subjects inside the frame: rendering those held by the frame essentially objects. From Edward S. Curtis, to the archive of *National Geographic*, to contemporary fashion modeling contracts, the photographer has been given narrative power and legal property over the represented subject. Through the law, the culture of the image making lies with the photographer, videographer, the manufacturer, creating a sociality where the people inside the frame are considered captured, owned, and material to be manipulated. In addition to the construction of the spectacle, relegating the power of creation solely with the photographer has harmed and violated the people that make the image possible. Such harmful understandings of authorship and ownership must be shattered.

Third, and carefully, I want to push against the consistent discourse of surprise within technological "advancements" and the gendered and racialized implications of their research. Explicit pornographic imagery did not arrive after the rise and through the boredom of the family portrait. The invention of pornographic imagery happened in tandem with the first realistic imaging technology: the invention of the daguerreotype. I situate this history not to collapse into a nihilistic fantasy of inevitability but in order to grapple with how dominant imaginaries become normalized via technology, and how moral outrage against them is not a site of contradiction, but how they're maintained. I do so in order to consider the space needed for the creation of more, and not less fantasy, and for a liberated understanding of the image.

*

## On the Real and the Fake

Philosophers, theorists and psychoanalysts have defined and refined the "real" and "truth" for over millennia with little resolve. At times the debates have spawned ongoing camps, such as Plato's idealism and Aristotle's realism. Other times it has defined new approaches to the world, such as Descartes' enlightenment proclamation "I think therefore I am," or as the mystery that remains unknown, such as Lacanian psychoanalysis and its insistence that the "real" exists but is out of reach.

Others, particularly in art, have called for the philosophical project of authenticity to be abandoned altogether. Deep fakes sprang into the world as the username of a Reddit user who created fake celebrity pornography using machine learning, and has since become synonymous with the usage of generative adversarial networks (GANs) to engineer representation. Previously, GANS served as the "creative" component for machine learning programs, where neural networks would make up data and other components to assist AI software in the absence of sufficient training materials. When launched on 2018 on Reddit, the technology composited celebrity faces to the bodies of unidentified non-celebrity women using machine learning, creating more "believable" and altered pornography. Reporting at the Association for Computing Machinery, the SIGGRAPH conference in 2018, VICE journalist Turton (2018) commented on the unanimous reception of deep fakes as one of surprise, "The researchers apparently hadn't considered how the technology they were developing could be misused." In contrast, creators of new popularized deep fakes have provided interviews describing that they want to "democratize" the tool, so that eventually technological knowledge will not be required to make such videos. Some of this software continues to remain readily available, free.[2] In this "democratization" deep fakes have been made of politicians and political speeches, celebrities being casted into different roles, spiraling debates as to whether or not we are moving into a future where we may never be able to "trust" what we see.

In a different vein, Art critic David Joselit questioned the critical powers of representation after the failure to indict a police officer for the murder of Eric Garner in 2014. Joselit (2015) compelling provokes how research and information-driven post-conceptual art must be reformulated if a witness can capture a murder on camera and it does not serve as proof. Has the thesis centralized in art making and representation – that seeing the world differently prompts transformation and reflection – been incorrect?

Joselit's charge tends to how notions of truth and its image do not exist in a vacuum, but require structural power and momentum. The continuum from fiction to reality is demonstrated by research into how repeated exposure to manipulation works to cement its authority.[3] In examining the dangers of deep fakes, legal scholars Chesney and Citron (2019) take up two hypothetical examples that hinge closely to similar events that have already occurred in the world. They ask readers to imagine a deepfake of Israeli soldiers murdering a Palestinian child, and a deepfake that enhances what the police may have done during the murder of Freddie Gray in Baltimore (p. 887). Considering that there exists an abundance of documentation of Israeli military violence in Gaza, and police violence toward Black persons remains ongoing in the United States, Chesney and Citron demonstrate how the operations of emerging technology expose the shallow depth of fakes, in that they would work to accelerate pre-established understandings of the world.

In contrast with the failure to indict Garner's murder irrespective of proof, consider the workings of state propaganda that effectively disseminated and enforced ideas that most now believe to be untrue. From figures such as Dr Seuss constructing imagery on behalf of the US military to conjure public support for the internment of Japanese Americans, to the CIA's establishment of the Congress for Cultural Freedom in the 1960s that worked to combat socialist aesthetics by promoting depoliticized US art as emblematic of US freedom, the label of "fake" does not remedy the historic and lasting harms harnessed in their structural formations.

Free speech apologists often cite this history in bad faith to dismiss the gravity of deep fakes. They comment on how fakes and their fictions have existed before and will continue to persist. And while it is true that doctored imagery has been around, exposure to them has created ongoing reverberations. We witness their continuance into this moment, from the narrative of the "savage" who must be colonized, to the consequences faced by those considered objects. Such fictions bring us to a realm where the filmed murder of Gardner fails to serve as proof of injustice.

Meaning is mediated and requires the affirmation of societal structures, in the form of education, publication, exposure and circulation. What rejectors of truth or libertarian arguments for limitless free speech evade are the powers of fiction, particularly when promulgated by state and structural forces. The fictions produced in society reveal what Marxist literary scholar Raymond Williams described as "structures of feeling" – the percolating desires and politics that have yet to find formed and clear language. This is discussed in criticisms of everything from the normalization of gendered and racialized violence on television, to science fiction's racist and colonial normalizations as articulated by NK Jemison and others, to the socialist futures foreclosed in blockbuster Hollywood films. Rather than as sources of radical imagination, mass produced forms of cultural fictions often ameliorated racial and misogynistic attitudes under the guise of "imaginary."

This contemporary moment is one held by the tension between those like Joselit who have argued that that the image is the limitation of truth, and the proliferation of images that claim to be real *and* fake.[4] Deep fakes demand that we grapple with how objectivity is our fantasy, the controls the narrative of objectivity an ongoing continual fight.

To create false representations of one's sexual fantasy, or to occupy a position of power that one does not have, speaks to the power of fiction in constructions of reality. That the first deployment of machine learning was used almost in a parallel fashion to the surgeon in *Boxing Helena* – to remove the autonomy of women as one's fantasy – speaks to this phenomena, as patriarchal objecthood remains seeped into the inner workings of cultural production and the law. That the second most circulated clip was the manipulation of the presidential position also demonstrates how popular fiction reifies recognized sources of power and authority, and offers at best, slight deviations.[5] Given the massive imaginative potential in machine learning technology, its execution thus far has affirmed preexisting structures in society, from corporate and state power to patriarchal and colonial narratives.

Thus, Golumbia (2009) argues against fixating on an emerging technology as the problem, or in explicating its novelty, and instead asks for the focus to be on the history, culture, politics that bring society to a moment in which these technologies amplify the preexisting societal inequities (p. 3). To hone in on the "novelty" of a particular tech is, he writes,

often based on willful avoidance of the existence of analogous phenomena in the recent historical past. Networks, distributed communication, personal involvement in politics, and the geographically widespread sharing of information about the self and communities have been characteristic of human societies in every time and every place.

(p. 3)

And if anything, such technologies unbearably highlight how, "the more things change, the more things stay the same" (p. 3). The emphasis on the emerging tech as the culprit elides how the tech is built upon the foundations of other tech, which is built in a culture that imagined and funded each stage of its development. Emergent technology such as AI generated representation is not contradictory to society, but rooted in it. Deep fakes are less about its unique technical intricacies and more about how the infrastructure required to remedy gendered and racialized violence does not exist in our digital, imaginary, and material worlds.

\*

## Photography and Constructions of the Human

In *Intimacies of Four Continents* Lowe (2015) argues how the conception of *human* was defined as white and European, in opposition to the enslaved and colonized (p. 3). This definition became transmuted into the realm of photography, where plantation owners, photographers and magazines affirmed colonial depictions of the human, as when colonized and Indigenous persons were depicted, they were done to affirm settler-colonial fantasies.

Such as the portraits manufactured by Edward S. Curtis. Sponsored by one of the richest financiers of his time, JP Morgan, and pre-emptively titled the "Vanishing Race," Curtis manipulated images of Indigenous persons as premodern, and rather than targets of genocide and dispossession, simply "disappearing." In studying Curtis archive, photo scholar Faris (2003) writes of how Curtis outfitted many of his sitters, posing them with additional jewelry from tribes to which they did not belong for dramatic "effect," or would remove watches and signs of "modernity," almost never printing images in which they smiled (though there were many), going as far as painting his nephew in redface. This was all done so that his images presented the people described by his title: as no longer alive but vanishing. In parallel fashion, when capturing enslaved persons, photographer Joseph Zealy removed their clothing, effectively staging nude scenes yet situating them to be authentic.[6] And contemporary magazines such as *National Geographic* have issued apologies for racist depictions that they described as "genuine" and "natural."[7] Though once billed as "real," these image outline the history of power, as significant financial capital investments, and technologies were developed to manufacture and circulate the colonial aesthetic.

As W.E.B. DuBois pointed out a hundred years ago, the function of the camera perpetuates racialized terror, and this function has not changed in the move toward digital technologies.[8] The legacy of the camera's colonial eye persists as digital cameras were built through the foundations laid out by analog technology. And everything from white balance to the operations of color prioritizes the imperial gaze of the camera. Former senior research scientist at Pixar, who worked on films such as: *Coco, Incredibles 2*, and *Toy Story 4*, and current professor of computer science at Yale University, Theodore Kim discusses this history. In a 2021 lecture on "Anti-Racist Graphics researcher" Kim delves into how the legacy of methods utilized in analog film, from 'leader ladies" – the white women who served as reference for color in film processing – to the fundamentals of lighting, such as background lighting aka "rim lighting" due to the light produced by blond hair transfer into digital technologies as problems of algorithm and software.[9] Kim (2020) argues how the construction of skin in fantasy films such as *Lord of the Rings* and *Harry Potter* equate to translucency, and like the whiteness of "leader ladies" of 35 mm film, the algorithms made to render skin has exclusively been designed for white persons; this tendency translates also into hair. Considering that the field of visual effects is compromised overwhelmingly of white men – 96% are white and 97% are male – the development of CGI for whiteness is not accidental.[10]

The racial segregation produced by technologies of representation is often dealt with in post-production. In "Looking at Shirley," Roth (2009) interviews TV cinematographers who discuss how the camera set to Whoopi Goldberg differed from the settings for her white counterparts, suggesting that the footage from multiple cameras was composited for her television show (p. 130). As in, multiple cameras were required: one for Goldberg and another for white counterparts. This is because the camera that can clearly see both Goldberg and her white counterparts does not exist. In order to present a unified frame, their frames were most likely layered together and composited.[11]

Compositing (or amputating, perhaps) is the processing site where frames are reconfigured, adjusted and rendered to enact the surface of a *complete* frame.[12] And outside of cinematographers, editors, compositors and those interested, it would be difficult to discern which have been altered this way. In the film industry this role is a unionized position: the compositors are credited by name. Without the presence of monsters on screen, or behind-the-scenes clips, if one wanted to deconstruct the constructions of the film/image, one could look through to see: the credited flame artists, the compositors or others in post-production, or search for behind-the-scenes footage in order to understand how the film was composited. In this learning it can be gathered that everything from historical dramas such as HBO's

*John Adams* to the film *Mean Girls* has been composited and manipulated in post-production. The composited frame that we see eventually on the screen – be it Goldberg, John Adams and more – are not called *fakes*. They are simply called television and film.

Commercial imaging enterprises operate through the promise and limitations of software.[13] Though newly "updated" cameras are produced, they do not amend their foundational racial imaging. Instead, it is simply understood as what the camera cannot do will be relegated to post-production.

The current components needed to create a deepfake are selected footage, a computer that can process machine learning, the ability to use the said program/app and the desire to create manipulated imaging. All parts are needed for its creation. It is in this vein that we can understand the structural formation of the deepfake, which is fundamentally about the function of post-production – which takes what the camera has already recorded – and considers it *raw* and manipulatable; deep fakes retell the story of how certain images, persons, depictions have become situated as raw.

Thus, to fixate only on the machine learning and software/app component would be to elide on what Golumbia prompted, which is its pre-established formations. As in, who is considered manipulatable and thus raw? What kinds of footage and imagery are considered *raw* and for the taking? What kinds of manipulations are desired? Who feels authorized to make them?

It is through these questions that we can understand the structural formation of the deepfake predicated upon the function of post-production – which takes what the camera has already recorded – and considers it *raw* and manipulatable.

Deep fakes retell the story of how certain images, persons, depictions have become situated as raw.

\*

## Raw Material

Speaking on the necessity to push against libertarian arguments for "free digital speech" that include deep fakes, legal scholars Franks and Waldman (2019) argue how "digitally manipulated pornography turns individuals into objects of sexual entertainment against their will (p. 893)."[14] As situated, the interplay between the freedoms of "artist subject" and the subject-turned-object has a long history that begins with the camera. On the interconnections between colonialism and photography, Azoulay (2021) describes [sic] the invention "as an imperial practice" that rendered those photographed "raw material." We can witness this dynamic playing out in many of the examples examined earlier – including the language of post-production, which describes images to be manipulated as "raw" – and we see this relegation into "raw" unfolding in contemporary legal practice.

In the 2019 legal symposium on deep fakes, Chesney and Citron note (2019) how civil litigation against their creation would likely be unfeasible. Though victims could sue creators of deep fakes for defamation, the individual would need to find the perpetrator, and then for jurisdictional reasons this entity would need to reside in the United States, not to mention the upfront investigative and legal costs of this endeavor. They situate how an alternative legal route might involve the deployment of criminal charges, as the First Amendment does not necessarily apply to impersonation, and thus, criminal impersonation laws could apply, "so long as law enforcement has training in the law and technology (pp. 889–890)" – which seems highly unlikely.

As cases against those who have distributed nonconsensual intimate images have demonstrated, photography laws privilege a narrow definition of photographer and owner.[15] Therefore, those seeking to halt the distribution of non-consensually distributed material are often unsuccessful on the grounds that they do not have property claims over images of their own body, and there is even less legal precedent providing justice to those who have been the target of doctored, fake imagery or the nonconsensual circulation of photographs, such as the portraits of Curtis or Zealy. Yet Chesney and Citron's interpretation of how impersonation and the criminal law could be utilized in the future is intriguing, given how current photography rulings have provided little protections to those inside the frame. A clear example of this is the ongoing lawsuit against Harvard University's ownership of the daguerreotypes of enslaved people.

Renty Taylor and Delia were the given names of enslaved persons in South Carolina; Ms. Tamara Lanier is a direct descendent of Renty Taylor. Harvard University currently owns daguerreotypes of Renty because the late eighteenth-century professor century Louis Agassiz – whose statue still decorates the campus and whose museum continues to this day – had them commissioned for a paper he was writing to oppose Darwin's theories of evolution. Akin to southern plantation owners, Agassiz advocated for polygenesis and believed in species separation. Thus, akin to the propagandic effect Curtis' images had in the US imaginary, images of Renty and Delia and others were procured from their enslavers and taken by Joseph Zealy so that Agassiz could argue that Black persons were not of the same species as white persons, and based on this premise, enslavement of them may be justified and miscegenation must not occur. Agassiz' students continued his research and extended his politics by advocating on behalf of legal segregation. His theories have been foundational to the usurpation of white supremacy as a serious form of scientific inquiry.

Currently, Ms. Lanier is asking that Harvard University relinquish ownership of the daguerreotypes. Harvard remain owners because of Agassiz and his collaboration with plantation owners. As Renty and Delia were enslaved, they were deprived of consent and property during the making of the images. Thus surely, one does not believe the images captured of them in support of polygenesis, which functioned to validate chattel slavery, are their *true* depictions? Surely, we might surmise that they are manipulated depictions in service of Agassiz' scientific racism – of polygenesis and the foundations for a white supremacist gaze? Might this too be considered a primary form of criminal impersonation?

The current answer is no. The case brought forth as a civil suit was dismissed before it could even be heard. In the 2021 dismissal of Lanier's petition (*Lanier* v. *Harvard*, 2021) to retrieve her enslaved ancestor's images from Harvard, Judge Camille Sarrouf wrote most plainly, "the court finds that Renty and Delia did not possess an interest in the photograph, and as a result, Lanier has no such interest" (p. 11). Could the current legal system accept the argument of criminal impersonation for others – persons who were and are not enslaved – given that Ms. Lanier's case was dismissed before a hearing could even be conducted?

I raise Chesney and Citron's gesture toward the potential of criminal law and impersonation, alongside the judge's dismissal, to tend to the current limits of the law and the questions raised by their limitations. Rather than taking into consideration that Renty and Delia were enslaved, the judge holds the history of their depravity into the present: "Renty and Delia did not possess an interest in the photograph, and as a result, Lanier has no such interest" (p. 11). This is akin to saying, because they were enslaved then, they cannot be free today: because the laws did not permit their freedom then, the law will not permit their freedom now. Because the laws upheld the property rights of the photographer and Agassiz and Harvard, who supported the dehumanization of Black enslaved persons then, the law will continue to uphold this rationale into the present.

To uphold her decision the judge cited a plethora of cases where photographers working for and behalf of states, prisons and corporations have been privileged over their non-consenting victims.[16] She points to such cases to say: the property remains with the photographer even when their subjects did not consent. And thus, the deprived consent of an enslaved person is leveled as akin to the deprived consent of victims *and* thus irrelevant.

That property claims have been provided to the photographer over the subject is a site of alarm. This is a law that privileges the technical knowledge and equipment of a white propertied class over the people who make the picture possible. It is as if the law considers ownership of equipment and technical capabilities as grounds to harm others and fundamentally denies what makes the image possible.

Photo history and copyright legislation already give rights to the photographer and not the subject in the frame, who is understood as an object within the frame.[17] This dynamic is amplified in the deepfake, within a culture where only the artist, the photographer, is entitled. Moreover, irrespective of how the law will slowly adjudicate deepfake provisions, much of US culture has adapted what has been normalized from photography. In this history and presence, it is more conceivable that the manipulation efforts of some will be privileged as creative above those who protest its manipulation. The people who make the images possible are denied property and consent. The work of the photographer/scientist is considered protected, and the image of those photographed is denied a value or a presence. They are in essence, raw, disregarded. This historical and continual disregard speaks to denial but not a disembodiment.

*

## Proposed Solutions

From the scientists who used photography as evidence in their arguments against miscegenation, to the development of what Roth delineates in "Shirley Cards," to the algorithms developed only for white skin in motion graphics, to Marriott's (2000) questions of the timing of 35 mm roll film and the circulation of lynching photography – the history of image technology reflects the oppressive power dynamics of white supremacy. The ability to control the image of certain groups and persons and thus control how reality is defined has too often been the goal of state and corporate power. As such, the history of manufactured objecthood, the prioritization of whiteness, came with the rise of US empire and its military.

In response to deep fakes, the US government, the Defense Advanced Research Projects Agency (DARPA), has spent over $68 million in two years on digital forensics that *might* be able to fight the emerging technology, and in 2019, the house passed the "Deepfake Report Act," which would [sic] "requires the Science and Technology Directorate in the Department of Homeland Security to report at specified intervals on the state of digital content forgery technology." And the report defines this forgery as "the use of emerging technologies, including artificial intelligence and machine learning techniques, to fabricate or manipulate audio, visual, or text content with the intent to mislead."[18] In a moment where those in government are there through the proliferation of fake news and alternative facts, such as the 45th presidency, it is unclear what kind of solution this bill and DARPA could provide.

Moreover, the history of CGI lies in the shared modern history of military developments that have since become popularized, personalized and turned into user-driven software. CGI is militarized knowledge[19] in that its omnipresence is unknown.[20] This is not the way corporate and military researchers would view this history, as they often posit a positive advancement narrative.

Legal scholars and policy experts have also advocated the use of "authentication" software, and countless forensic companies have been launched in this service. Chesney and Citron (2019) note how authentication software, however, may not be as useful if digital platforms do not also use them.[21] Either way, situating newer and better software as providing a solution to a problem generated by the over-dependence and reliance on technologies of racialized and colonial sight ensures that the structural root of the problem will remain unaddressed.

Additionally, much like other forms of technology, detecting its "faults" works in its developmental aid. When it was reported that deep fakes can be spotted by blinking and eye movement inconsistencies, the next batch of videos and software addressed the issue.[22] If social media and software usage have taught us anything about technology, it is that reporting the error, crash or problem is a form of alienated labor that improves the tech. Thus, if finding the flaw ameliorates it, if the function of mastery is its illusory – which is that knowledge accelerates and mutates by design and in accordance to societal forces – it would be important to focus on its societal design.

Unlike what neoliberalism advocates, user empowerment rarely amounts to greater freedom. Rather, as Chun (2011) suggests, software functions as a key metaphor of neoliberalism, of the individual who must empower themselves with more knowledge in order to better navigate the system. If better "empowerment" – spotting its false cues, seams and pointing them out – aids in their acceleration, if criticism of them and laws against becomes the opportunity to grow another loop, if "knowledge" – understanding how they're made – aids in their normalization, we become stuck inside the primary function of software: which conceives of all the possibilities and creates clear limits for our routes beforehand and asks us to be *creative* within them. If we are to truly disrupt the depth of machine learning–generated fakes, we must go beyond the program, to the hardware, to their material resources.

Crawford (2021) argues that machine learning is not just an abstract black box algorithm unknowable and mysterious to those outside of those who write them but embodied by the minerals, resources and processes required to sustain and run them. The embodiment of AI – as processes of the earth – speaks to the impact of deep fakes as material. In fact, the embodiment of machine learning is a clear box, where its targets, powers and impact have been made transparent. Its "black boxing" invention is part of an imagination privileged in society, and its execution "clear box" are its embodied tools, to which the impact cannot be denied. The person who is augmenting and the software they use is connected to the life of this world. Crawford argues how tech companies often deploy the language of carbon neutral and tout environmental concerns in advocating for the growth of digital realms. This language and argument are often accepted without contestations because of what Jurgenson (2011) describes as "digital dualism" wherein "life" and the "real" become split from what occurs "digitally" – much like the tradition of the Enlightenment sought to do by splitting the mind from the body. The digital in many ways occupies what is considered to be immaterial. And just like the ideologies advanced by immaterialist discourse, it evades the materiality of its construction.[23]

Currently, AI is exclusively extractive, and imagined "better uses" do not mitigate the vast ecological destruction that occurs under its domain. Aside from the fact that what happens "digitally" is always embodied because it requires our presence, memories, labor, the labor of others and our lives, the digital realm is predicated upon a vast amount of extracted resources and fundamentally contributes greatly to environmental decline.[24] "Virtual" spaces such as data centers, products such as Bitcoin and other digital processes require immense amounts of electricity. And in this, machine learning researcher Emma Strubell reports that when calculating natural language processing – interactions between computers and human language pivotal to AI design – "only a single NLP (natural language processing) model produced more than 660,000 pounds of carbon dioxide emissions (p. 42)," and these are considered extremely conservative estimates.[25]

In speaking to the processing power of maintaining a database, to running machine learning algorithms and programs, it is safe to agree with Crawford in that far from immaterial, our digital activities become *what the planet does*. Each command marks a material imprint onto the planet. These imprints, from harvesting the minerals that are required to build the machines, to the generation of electricity and more, are irreversible. This is to say, in addition to the gravity of fake imagery in place of our real, we – all of us living and that will be living on this planet – will witness the weight of their embodiment through the degradation of our environment. When we discuss deep fakes, we should do so with this in mind: that the fakes are the embodiment of systems that structured whiteness and coloniality into the image/sight, the embodiment of a legal system that privileged technical ownership and use and authorized the transfiguration from subjects to objects, that these notions were enforced by the state, and this was reflected in how photographers, artists and scientists crafted representations and narratives about truth, which becomes embodied by earth in the quest to create better fakes of this world. Thus, a transformation in truth and its image will require a foundational breaking from this embodiment.

Situating the key component that differentiate deep fakes – it is machine learning – not to the site of the unknown program but as the embodiment of the earth is vital to reorienting the problem as not *out there* but *in here*. Likewise, legal theorists Silbey and Hartzog (2019) argue that the one "upside" of the deepfake is the "opportunity for repair" (p. 960). Writing, "an effective way to respond to the scourge of deep fakes isn't to target the creation and use of deep fakes themselves, but rather to focus on strengthening the social and political institutions they disrupt." As "Journalism, education, individual rights, democratic systems, and voting protocols have long been vulnerable (960)." The threats new technology pose are manifestations of the brokenness of preexisting and established social infrastructure. How to address the "new" developments in tech with more "new" tech is a way not to address the structural problems at hand but to elude or, at worst, accelerate them. The logic that technology is changing society elides how society is the world; rather than fixating one part of the technology, I ask that we begin by questioning how does the world change?

*

To conclude, I want to discuss the gendered formations embedded into imaging, and how image technology manifests through constructions of gendered desire. As discussed, from its onset, cameras have been producers of altered imaging, and the history of photography is the material history of developments in post-production, from color processing to compositing. The fact that deep fakes have been deployed to perpetuate gendered violence is not surprising – it is a testament to the ongoing domination of patriarchy and misogyny within how neoliberal technology is imagined, developed and deployed. While tending to how deep fakes and photography have been consistently used as a weapon of gendered and racialized violence, I want to try and reconfigure the discussion on representation and imaging outside the residual truth claims embedded in the language of the real, as its definition is beholden to a technology of colonial systems that must be abolished. The presence of deep fakes pries open a future, present and past in which the fake becomes undetectable. How do we – those invested in a truth claim, in justice – grapple with the settling of the simulacra? Through a disavowal of present systems, how might the simulacra be unsettled? This is not a statement about giving up on the real/truth, but as anti-colonial and anti-capitalists struggles have demonstrated, *truth* is an ongoing process that must be fought again and again.

Invented in France during the mid-nineteenth century, the first camera the daguerreotype was first widely used to document European royalty and beauty. Solomon-Godeau (1986) writes about one of the daguerreotype's first practitioners of self-portraiture, Countess Castiglione, who used the technology to recreate images of past ball entrances. In writing about how the Countess manipulated the images to make herself appear younger and more beautiful, Godeau argues that the Countess' archive displays her contribution to Empire *with* the limitations of femininity. Though it is surmised that the images the Countess created were private and solely for her use, they also reflect how the Countess understood the desires others had of and for her. Particularly, the Countess photographed parts of herself, often her bare legs, emulating the images sold of ballerinas and sex workers.

In situating the sexualization of bare legs, Solomon-Godeau demonstrates how explicit sexual imagery is not a contemporary phenomenon but a priori to imaging. She charts how the minute daguerreotypes were invented, explicit nude and images documenting sex acts were produced and hidden in pocket watches, jewelry boxes and other kinds of concealed compartments. Though it is often argued that new technology corrupts understandings of the heteronormative family and augments "traditional" understandings of sex, it is useful to know that pornographic imagery has existed from the beginning of the camera. With this established, Solomon-Godeau subtly questions the images the Countess produced of herself and her body in private. In her private self-representation, she demonstrated her understanding of hegemonic fantasy and desire. Though a Countess, she openly yet secretly sexualized herself, photographing her legs, a practice now considered uncontroversial but then considered tawdry. She draped curtains around her body to make herself appear thinner and used analog post-production such as shading and coloring to make herself appear more youthful. Did she interpolate the gaze of others even when they were nowhere to be found? From the daguerreotype to the deepfake, one can trace how the history of race, gender and sight is constitutive with the structures of power, surveillance and fantasy. Whose fantasy becomes represented – in public and private – time and time again?

Brown and Fleming (2020) argue that whiteness and white power operate *as* the deepfake, and use renditions of {Schar-JØ} (deep fakes with the head of the actress Scarlett Johannsson) to demonstrate this point. Brown and Fleming tend to the unidentified actresses whose bodies become attached to the heads of celebrities. Their bodies are necessary to the spectacle, and yet the removal of their bodily autonomy has received almost no attention or analysis. This is curious, given how the violation deployed against the anonymized bodies is considerable. If we are to surmise that the footage of the sex acts were consensually circulated, perhaps as paid sex work, then the deepfake removes the agency of the actor and the labor and renders both inconsequential. In effect, Brown and Fleming are accurate in assessing this dispossession as the operations of white power. The deepfake is a continuation of the fantasy of dispossession, where subjects can be transmute into objects, highlighting how hyper-visibility and invisibility become weaponized against the other, creating a hierarchy of grievance and horror: from the face, to the headless body, from the voice and the labor removed of repulsion, ambivalence or desire, held hostage by the repeating mise-en-scène of the another.

*

In a system in which emerging visual technology exemplifies the imagination of the dominant forms, and the person inside the frame is considered an object, how might we advocate for more fantasy, and not less?

Within the tradition of photography Azoulay (2020) suggests a "non-imperial understanding" of it, where authorship is not so clearly defined with one photographer but where "The encounter involves not only the one who holds the camera and those in front of it, but also other participants, including imaginary spectators." Azoulay outlines the possibility where image technology is the starting, and not concluding, point for the imaginary. What might it be to make representations with shared understanding, knowing that negotiations of their terms will be ongoing? Where the image recorded is but one facet of the encounter, and no one with memories of the encounter – from those inside the frame to imaginary spectators – are considered object?

In *Boxing Helena*, Helena is a captured object who bitches. As the object trapped in a box, she remains indignant, belittling, foul. Poet and essayist June (2003) speaks to this phenomenon. While acknowledging the overwhelming presence of state, white supremacists and anti-Black violence, she presses:

> We are not powerless. We are indispensable despite all atrocities of state and corporate policy to the contrary. At a minimum we have the power to stop cooperating with our enemies. We have the power to stop the courtesies and to let the feelings be real. . . . At the very least, if we cannot control things we certainly can mess them up.

Deepfake technology is embodied and reflects the most pressing concerns of the world. Everything that happens in digital spaces happens because it has already occurred *here* – this is shared space. Thus, until emergent image technology can break from its colonial foundation (which means, until *this space* can be ruptured) to become more than another tool of domination, and even then, perhaps some of us are ungrateful and disobedient. Perhaps the delinquency mutates and capitulation becomes wholly refused.

This is my fantasy and so, perhaps.

## Acknowledgment

I thank Michael Filimowicz for inviting me to contribute to this volume and for organizing and editing this collection. An early version of this chapter was presented in 2018 at the American Studies conference in Atlanta as part of the "Technological Emergence and Political Emergencies at the Intersection of Race, Gender, and Resistance" panel organized by Neda Atanasoski and Kalindi A Vora. Casey Boyle read early drafts of this chapter, and Fatima El-Tayeb has been my interlocutor in thinking through race and the image. I thank them for their questions, insights and critiques.

## Notes

1  I thank Casey Boyle for bringing this filmic parallel to my attention.
2  L. Whittaker, T. C. Kietzmann, J. Kietzmann and A. Dabirian, explain how effective this software has become, writing, "Using free software called Deep-FaceLab and only seven days, one YouTuber recreated Netflix's de-aging effects and released a video comparing the CGI of the actors within scenes from The Irishman to the deepfake version of the actors. The deepfake recreation of the scenes was highly convincing and has even been hailed as superior to the costly CGI effects, which were reported as being "distractingly bad" and like "some hellish uncanny valley"; see (2020). "All Around Me are Synthetic Faces": The Mad World of AI-Generated Media, *IT Professional*, 22(5).
3  "Knowledge Does Not Protect Against Illusory Truth" refutes this truism in their study, writing, [c]ontrary to prior suppositions, illusory truth effects occurred even when participants knew better." See L. K. Fazio, N. M. Brashier, B. K. Payne, & E. J. Marsh (2015). Knowledge Does not Protect Against Illusory Truth, *Journal of Experimental Psychology*, 144(5), 993–1002. Also, J. Concha (2018, June 18). Pew Study Finds Americans Can't Tell Fact from Opinion. *The Hill*. https://thehill.com/homenews/media/392870-pew-study-fmds-americans-cant-tell-fact-from-opin- ion.
4  For an exploration on the other side of Joselit, see F. Foer (2018, May). *The Atlantic*. www.theatlantic.com/magazine/archive/2018/05/realitys-end/556877/.
5  Such as Jordan Peele's deepfake as Obama. See C. Silverman (2018, April 17). How to Spot a Deepfake Like the Barack Obama – Jordan Peele Video. *Buzzfeed*. www.buzzfeed.com/craigsilverman/obama-jordan-peele-deepfake-video-debunk-buzzfeed.
6  For an in-depth analysis of the daguerreotypes, see M. Fox-Amato (2019). *Exposing Slavery: Photography, Human Bondage, and the Birth of Modern Visual Politics in America*. Oxford University Press.
7  For the full statement, see S. Goldberg (2018, March 12). From the Editor: Race, Racism, History. *National Geographic*. www.nationalgeographic.com/magazine/article/from-the-editor-race-racism-history.
8  W.E.B. Du Bois wrote in *Crisis*, 1923, "Why do not more young colored men and women take up photography as a career? The average white photographer does not know how to deal with colored skins and having neither sense of the delicate beauty or tone nor will to learn, he makes a horrible botch of portraying them."

9  For the full lecture, see T. Kim (2021) *Anti-Racist Graphics Research* (SIGGRAPH 2021). www.youtube.com/watch?v=ROuE8xYLpX8&t=2547s&ab_channel =TheodoreKim.

10 For a breakdown of race and the film industry, see J. Loftus (2015, February 20). An Illustrated Breakdown of the Not-So-Diverse Oscar Voters. *BCDWire*. www. bdcwire.com/oscar-voter-diversity/

11 W.R. Booth is said to have invented compositing in 1901 for The Haunted Curiosity Shop. For full timeline of visual effects, see B. Flueckiger (2011, January). *History of Visual Effects VFX, Computer Graphics, CGI, Computer Animation. Visual Effects Timeline*. www.zauberklang.ch/timeline.php.

12 I have written about the intersections between compositing and the human; see (2016). CGI Monstrosities: Modernist Surfaces, the Composite and the Making of the Human Form, in *Reading Modernism with Machines*, eds. Ross, S., & O'Sullivan, J. Palgrave Macmillan Press, pp. 265–290.

13 W. Chun (2011) argues, "Race and software therefore mark the contours of our current understanding of visual knowledge as "programmed visions." See, *Programmed Visions Software and Memory*, MIT Press, 2011.

14 Franks and Waldman analyze libertarian arguments situating how, "Civil libertarians argue that revenge porn, fake news, and other forms of bad speech are part of the price we pay for a free society."

15 For an example of cases and legal arguments on how the nonconsensual circulation of images have been enacted, see D. Citron & M. Franks (2014). Criminalizing Revenge Porn. *Wake Forest Law Review*, 49, 345–383.

16 In (*Lanier* v. *Harvard*, 2021) Judge Sarrouf writes, "It is basic tenet of common law that the subject of a photograph has no interest in the negative or any photographs printed from the negative, see Thayer v. Worcester Post Co., 284 Mass. 160, 163–164 (1933); rather the negative and any photographs are the property of the photographer. Ault v. Hustler Magazine, 860 F. 2d 877, 883 (9th Cir. 1988). This principle is true even where an image is taken without the subject's consent. See United States v. Jiles, 658 F. 2d 194, 200 (3rd Cir. 1981) (holding juvenile did not show he was deprived of property interest when photograph was taken while in custody); Berger v. Hanlon, 1996 U.S. Dist LEXIS 225 at *30-*32 (D. Mont. 1996) (rejecting conversion claim against CNN for images taken without consent on property raided by FBI); Zacchini v. Scripps-Howard Broad. Co., 47 Ohio St. 2d 224, 227 (1976), rev'd on other ground, 433 U.S. 562 (1977) ("[I]t has never been held that one's countenance or image is 'converted' by being photographed.")

17 It's important to note that the cases upholding Harvard's claims are lawsuits brought against state and corporate entities, by incarcerated and wronged persons. I can imagine someone pointing out how the police do not like to be filmed and have objected to being filmed, and thus, perhaps current photo law protects the activist photographer. This is, unfortunately a misreading the current function of the law. See, B. Frazelle (2019, May 31). The Supreme Court Just Made It Easier for Police to Arrest You for Filming Them. *Slate*. https://slate.com/news-and-politics/2019/05/supreme-court-nieves-police-abuse-case.html.

18 For coverage of this spending, see S. Kampf & M. Kelley (2018, November 18). A New "Arms Race": How the U.S. Military is Spending Millions to Fight Fake Images. *CBC*. www.cbc.ca/news/science/fighting-fake-images-military-1.4905775. For the full bill, see 116th Congress, (2019, Oct 24). "S. 2065 Deepfake Report Act of 2019"

19  Much has also been written on the "military-entertainment complex" (See authors such as Tim Lenoir, Henry Lowod, Simon Penny) with CGI and war simulation (Sara Brady, Ian Bogost, Nina Huntemann, Matthew Kirschenbaum).

20  There are activists and scholars have done tremendous work around the omnipresence of militarization. For example, Network of Concerned Anthropologists (2009). *The Counter-Counterinsurgency Manual, Or, Notes on Demilitarizing American Society*. Prickly Paradigm Press. And C. Lutz, ed. (2009). *The Bases of Empire: The Global Struggle against U.S. Military Posts*. Pluto Press.

21  They write, "We should be watching advances in authentication technologies. Companies like Truepic are working on methods of authentication. If those methods are adopted broadly (a big "if"), it would help quickly authenticate content. The problem is that platforms are likely to continue posting content with few restrictions on provenance . . . because forensic technology is engaged in an arms race, there is little reason to place our hopes on a slam-dunk technical solution."

22  S. Lyu (2018, August 29). Detecting "Deepfake" Videos in the Blink of an Eye. *The Conversation*. https://theconversation.com/detecting-deepfake-videos-in-the-blink-of-an-eye-101072.

23  My forthcoming book *The Politics of Collecting: Race, Property & Aesthetic Formation* addresses the materiality of immaterialism.

24  In "Assessing ICT global emissions footprint: Trends to 2040 & recommendations" Lotfi and Elmeligi write, "ICT (Information and Communication Technology) GHGE relative contribution could grow from roughly 1–1.6% in 2007 to exceed 14% of the 2016-level worldwide GHGE by 2040, accounting for more than half of the current relative contribution of the whole transportation sector." B. Lotfi & A. Elmeligi (2018, March 10). *Journal of Cleaner Production*, 177(10), 448–463. https://doi.org/10.1016/j.jclepro.2017.12.239.

25  Crawford (2021) writes: "One of the early papers in this field came from AI researcher Emma Strubell and her team at the University of Massachusetts Amherst in 2019. With a focus on trying to understand the carbon footprint of natural language processing (NLP) models, they began to sketch out potential estimates by running AI models over hundreds of thousands of computational hours . . . initial numbers were striking. Strubell's team found that running only a single NLP model produced more than 660,000 pounds of carbon dioxide emissions, the equivalent of five gas-powered cars over their total lifetime (including their manufacturing) or 125 round-trip flights from New York to Beijing.
Worse, the researchers noted that this modeling is, at minimum, a baseline optimistic estimate."

## Works Cited

Azoulay, A. (2020, March 12). It is not Possible to Decolonize the Museum without Decolonizing the World. *Guernica Magazine*. www.guernicamag.com/miscellaneous-files-ariella-aisha-azoulay

Brown, W., & Fleming, D. H. (2020). Celebrity Headjobs: Or Oozing Squid Sex with a Framed-Up Leaky {Schar-JØ}. *Porn Studies*, 7(14), 357–366. https://doi.org/10.1080/23268743.2020.1815570

Chesney, R., & Citron, D. (2019). 21st Century-Style Truth Decay: Deep Fakes and the Challenge for Privacy, Free Expression, and National Security. *Maryland Law Review*, 78(4), 882–891.

Chun, W. (2011). *Programmed Visions Software and Memory*. MIT Press.

Crawford, K. (2021). *Atlas of AI Power, Politics, and the Planetary Costs of Artificial Intelligence*. Yale University Press.

Faris, J. (2003). Navajo & Photography. In Pinney, C., & Peterson, N. (eds.), *Photography's Other Histories*. Duke University Press.

Franks, M., & Waldman, A. (2019). Sex, Lies, and Videotape: Deep Fakes and Free Speech Delusions. *Maryland Law Review*, 78(4), 892–898.

Golumbia, D. (2009). *The Cultural Logic of Computation*. Harvard University Press.

Joselit, D. (2015). Material Witness: Visual Evidence and the case of Eric Gardner. *Artforum*, 53(6).

June, J. (2003). *Some of Us did not Die: New and Selected Essays*. Basic Books.

Jurgenson, N. (2011, February 24). Digital Dualism vs. Augmented Reality. *The Society Pages*. https://thesocietypages.org/cyborgology/2011/02/24/digital-dualism-versus-augmented-reality/

Kim, T. (2020, August 8). The Racist Legacy of Computer Generated Humans. *Scientific American*. www.scientificamerican.com/article/the-racist-legacy-of-computer-generated-humans/

Lanier, Tamara vs. President and Fellows of Harvard College Also Known as Harvard Corporation et al. (M.A. No. 2021-P-0350 (11)). www.mass.gov/doc/tamara-lanier-v-president-and-fellows-of-harvard-college-et-al-sjc-13138/download

Lowe, L. (2015). *Intimacies of Four Continents*. Duke University Press.

Marriott, D. (2000). *On Black Men*. Columbia University Press.

Roth, L. (2009). Looking at Shirley, the Ultimate Norm: Colour Balance, Image Technologies, and Cognitive Equity. *Canadian Journal of Communication*, 34(1), 111–136. https://doi.org/10.22230/cjc.2009v34n1a2196

Silbey, J., & Hartzog, W. (2019). The Upside of Deep Fakes. *Maryland Law Review*, 78(4), 960–966.

Solomon-Godeau, A. (1986, Winter). The Legs of the Countess. *October*, 39, 65–108.

Turton, W. (2018, August 27). 'Deepfake' Videos Like that Gal Gadot Porn are Only Getting More Convincing – and More Dangerous. *Vice*. www.vice.com/en/article/qvm97q/deepfake-videos-like-that-gal-gadot-porn-are-only-getting-more-convincing-and-more-dangerous

# Index

Adobe After Effects 7
Agassiz, Louis 59–60
Ahmed, S. 39
AI Singapore 37
Alphabet 4
Amazon 17
analog technology 57
Apple 17
Arendt, H. 41
artificial intelligence (AI): audio
    manipulations and 7–8; carbon
    footprint of 63, 69n25; cyberattacks
    and 9; deepfakes and 1, 5–9, 15,
    24–25; deep learning and 6, 24;
    ecological destruction and 63,
    69n24; embodiment of 62–64; fake
    pornography and 7; GANs and 6,
    24–25, 28–30; shallow fakes and
    7–8; social engineering techniques
    and 28; synthetic media and 23–24;
    systems of objectification and x, xi;
    virtual celebrities and 26
Asia: deepfake activity in 29–31;
    deepfake detection and 37–38;
    deepfake legislation and 35–36;
    disinformation campaigns and
    29–31; disinformation services in
    31–32; education efforts in 36–37;
    influence campaigns in 30; media
    literacy efforts 36–37, 39–40;
    shallow fakes in 32–35; synthetic
    media apps and services in 31;
    targeting of women politicians in 30
Association for Computing Machinery 53
audio manipulations 7–8, 26, 61
Aung San Suu Kyi 34

authentication software 19, 62, 69n21
authenticity: cognitive bias and 39;
    deepfake disruption to 29, 31, 36,
    38; detector misidentification of 38;
    documentary films and 8; philosophy
    of 53; public ability to discern 29,
    36, 41n5; public doubt in 31, 38
authority 34, 54, 67n3
Ayyub, Rana 30
Azoulay, A. 58, 66

Barthes, R. 13
Basuki Tjahaja Purnama 34
Baudrillard, J. 13–14
Beckham, David 26
Bharatiya Janata Party (BJP) 30
Bitcoin 5, 63
Bongo, Ali 29
Booth, W. R. 68n11
Bosworth, A. 11
bots 15, 33
Bourdain, Anthony 8
Boxing Helena x, 50–51, 55, 66
Brexit 10
Brown, W. 65–66
Buzzfeed 24

Cambridge Analytica 10–11
Carlson, M. 8
Castells, M. 3, 16
Cek Fakta 37, 40
celebrities: AI-created 26; deepfakes
    and 6, 25, 27, 29, 37; face-swap
    videos and 24–25, 53–54, 65;
    fake pornography and 50–51, 53;
    synthetic audio and 8

Centre on AI and Robotics 9

CGI *see* computer-generated imagery (CGI)

Chesney, R. 29, 54, 59–60, 62

China 30, 33–36

Chun, W. 62, 68n13

Citron, D. 54, 59–60, 62

Citron, D. K. 29

clickbait 14

compositing 57–58, 64, 68n11, 68n12

computer-generated imagery (CGI): compositing and 52; film industry and 51, 67n2; militarization and 69n20; military-entertainment complex and 69n19; racialized image-making and 52; synthetic media and 42n8; whiteness and 57

consumers of online content: awareness of deepfakes 23; deepfake detection and 17, 37–38, 62; deepfake sharing and 9–10, 14; digital literacy and x, 12–13; educational strategies for 12–13; meaning-making and 13–14; memes and 31; virtual silos and 15–16

copyright law 17, 51–52, 61

COVID-19 pandemic 23

Crawford, K. 62–63, 69n25

Cruise, Tom 23–24, 27, 37–38, 42n8

cultural fictions 55

Curtis, Edward S. 52, 56, 59

cyberbullying 35

cybercrime 9, 26, 29, 41

Cyberspace Administration of China (CAC) 35–36


daguerreotypes 53, 59–60, 65, 67n6

Dali Museum 5

DeepFace Lab 6, 67n2

deepfake pornography *see* fake pornography

Deepfake Report Act 61

deepfakes: AI technology and 1, 5–9, 15, 24–25; automated distribution of 1, 5; colonial imaginations and 51–52; cybercrime and 8–9, 26, 41; definition of 24; detection of 9, 17, 37–38, 40, 61–62; discrediting of authority and 34, 54; disinformation and 2, 23, 27–28; dispossession and 65–66; disruption of authenticity and 29, 31; educational strategies for 12–13, 36–37; embodiment of 63–64, 66; face-swap videos and 5, 24; fake news and 1–2, 42n9, 61; film and gaming industry 5, 26, 51; gendered violence and 50–51, 64; impact on public trust x, 1–2, 15, 29, 31, 34–35, 38, 41; influence of 7, 26–27; information disorder and 1–2, 15, 18; legislative strategies for 26, 35, 59, 61; misinformation and 5, 38; publicly available imagery and 6; puppet-master 24; racialized violence and 64; rise of 25–26; social media bans on 9–10; subject-turned-object in 51; targeting of politicians in 30–31; taxonomy on 38–39; technology-based solutions 19; weaponization of 7–8, 12, 35, 41; *see also* fake pornography; synthetic media

deep learning x, 6, 24–25, 32, 36

Deep Nude 29

Defense Advanced Research Projects Agency (DARPA) 61

Delia (enslaved person) 59–60

democracy 3, 15, 36

Derakhshan, H. 2

Descript 7

detection technology 37–38, 40, 61

digital democracy 15

digital dualism 63

digital literacy x, 12–13, 15, 18; *see also* media literacy

digital media: accelerated production of 50; amplification of social inequities and 55–56; colonial aesthetic and 56–57, 62, 66; corporate responsibility and 19; cultural architecture of 50–51, 56, 66; disinformation and 14–15; fake news and 4, 14; gendered violence and 55–56; lack of editorial oversight 3–5; mal-information and 14–15; misinformation and 14–15; network society and 16; neutrality of 8, 11–12; public trust in 16; racial imaging and 58, 68n13;

racialized violence and 55–56, 62;
reality effect of 13; regulation of 8,
12, 15–19, 51–52; societal design
and 16–17, 62, 64; spreadable
media and 3; superior knowledge
and 50; user empowerment and 62;
user-generated content 3–5, 14, 51;
whiteness and 57
Digital Millennium Copyright Act
(DMCA) 4
disinformation: COVID-19 pandemic
and 23; de-contextualized media
and 14; deepfakes and 2, 23, 27–28;
definition of 2, 41n1; digital media
and 14–15; global services for
31–32; hate speech and 33–34,
41n3; manipulation of online content
2; search engine manipulation and
2; social harm and 19; social media
and 1–2, 8
disinformation campaigns 27–31, 34
DuBois, W. E. B. 57, 67n8

e-commerce 3
Edgett, S. 11
Elmeligi, A. 69n24
enslaved persons 59–60
Epoch Media Group 27
Ethereum 5

FaceApp 29
Facebook: content authentication and
10; disinformation campaigns and
27–28; fake personas on 28, 30;
interventions in malicious content
17; lack of content oversight 4, 8,
11–12; micro-targeting of voters
10–11; misinformation and 33;
protection of advertising revenue
12; regulation of 12; removal of
deepfakes 37, 41n7; scale of content
creation 4; stance as neutral forum
4, 11–12
face-swap videos 5–7, 24–25,
53–54, 65
fake 53–55
FakeApp 6
Fake-Buster 37
fake faces 23, 28
fake news 1–2, 4, 15, 42n9, 61

fake pornography: AI technology
and 7; celebrities and 50–51, 53;
cybercrime and 29; face-swapping
and 25; nonconsensual images and
58–59, 65–66; objectification of
women and 7, 25; publicly available
imagery and 25; social media bans
on 9–10; targeting of professional
women 30; weaponization of 7–8, 25
Faris, J. 56
Ferreira, G. M. 3
film industry: audio manipulations
and 8; compositing and 57–58, 64,
68n11; deepfake technology and 5,
26, 51, 67n2; power of fiction and
55; race and 51, 55, 57–58, 68n10
Fleming, D. H. 65–66
Franks, M. 58, 68n14
free speech 10–12, 54–55, 58

Gadot, Gal 25
gaming industry 5
GANs *see* generative adversarial
networks (GANs)
Garner, Eric 54–55
gendered violence 50–51, 55–56, 64
generative adversarial networks
(GANs): celebrity pornography and
53; detection difficulties and 25,
30; neural network processes and 6,
24–25; synthetic profile photos and
28–30
Gif 10
Goldberg, Whoopi 57
Golumbia, D. 55
Google: celebrity footage on 25;
interventions in malicious content
17; lack of content oversight 4, 8,
12; reverse image searching and 40;
search engine volume 4; stance as
neutral platform 4, 11
Gov 2.0 Summit 18
Gray, Freddie 54
Gyfcat 10

Hartzog, W. 12, 64
Harvard University 59–60, 68n17
Haugen, Frances 12
human concept 56, 68n12
hyperreality 13–14

image literacy 13
images: anonymized bodies and 65–66; colonial aesthetic and 66; commercial enterprises 58; compositing and 57–58, 64; copyright law and 51; fake personas and 28; gendered formations and 51, 64; meaning-making and 13–14; nonconsensual 58–61, 68n15, 68n16; photographer rights and 51–53, 59–61, 68n16, 68n17; pornographic 53, 65; racialized 51–52, 56–58; reality effect of 13; settler-colonial fantasies and 56; structural power and 56, 58; subject as raw material 58–61, 68n16; white power and 65–66; widespread distribution of 14; *see also* digital media; photography
India 7, 15, 29–30, 33, 37
Indigenous persons 52, 56
Indonesia 34, 36–37, 40
*In Event of Moon Disaster* 8
influence campaigns 27–33
information disorder: deepfakes and 1–2, 15, 18; educational strategies for 15; fake news and 1; institutional resiliency and 2; legislative strategies for 15; response to 5, 15; shallow fakes and 7
Instagram 17
International Fact Checking Network 37, 40
*Intimacies of Four Continents* (Lowe) 56
Ipsos Singapore 42n9

Japan 29
Jemison, N. K. 55
Johannsson, Scarlett 65
Jones, Katie 28
Joselit, D. 54–55
journalism: crisis mode reporting on deepfakes 8; deepfake detection and 40; expert fact-checking and 40; fake identities and 28; media literacy efforts 36–37; platformization of newsrooms and 4; public trust in 35, 40; targeting of women in 30; veracity of information and 8;

vulnerability to fake news 1–5; *see also* news media
June, J. 66
Jurgenson, N. 63

KaiCatch 37
Kapwing 37
Kim, E. x
Kim, Jong Un 36
Kim, Theodore 57
Korea Advanced Institute of Science and Technology (KAIST) 37

Lanier, Tamara 59–60
legacy media *see* traditional media
legislation: clash with free speech 10, 54–55; copyright 51, 61; criminal impersonation and 59–60; deepfake regulation and 26, 35–36, 59, 61; information disorder and 15; new technologies and 8, 15, 51–52; social media and 17–18; tech sector responsibilities and 10, 17
liar's dividend 29
libertarianism 18, 55, 58, 68n14
LinkedIn 28
lip-sync 24
"Looking at Shirley" (Roth) 57
Lotfi, B. 69n24
Lowe, L. 56
Lynch, Jennifer 50

machine learning: AI technology and 5–6; artificial neural networks and 24, 52; deep learning and 6; embodiment of 62–64; generative adversarial networks (GAN) and 6; image datasets and 6; objectification of women and 55; power of fiction and 55
MAFINDO 36
Maher, S. x
mal-information 2, 14–15, 19
Marriott, D. 61
media: AI technology and x–xi; authenticity and 29; hyperpartisan consumption of 15; hyperreality and 13–14; public trust in x, 1–2, 15, 29, 34, 40; *see also* digital media; news media; synthetic media; traditional media

media literacy 36–37, 39–40; *see also* digital literacy
memes 14, 31
militarization 61–62, 69n20
military-entertainment complex 69n19
misinformation: COVID-19 pandemic and 23; de-contextualized media and 14; deepfakes and 5, 38; definition of 2, 41n1; digital media and 14–15; incitement to violence and 33; loss of trust in information 15; shallow fakes and 33–34; social harm and 19; social media and 33–34; violence and 33–34
misogyny 7, 50, 55, 64
MIT Center for Advanced Virtuality 8
Mueller, Robert 12
Mueller Report 12, 17
Murmu, Chandrani 30
Myanmar 31, 33–34

National Defense Authorization Act 2020 (NDAA) 35
*National Geographic* 52, 56
national security x, 27, 36
natural language processing (NLP) 63, 69n25
neoliberalism 62, 64
network society 3, 15–16, 19
Newberry, C. 4
Newman, E. J. 39
news media: authentication of 4; crisis mode reporting on deepfakes 8; impact of deepfakes on 1–2; legacy media 3–4; public trust in x, 1–4, 29, 31, 34; regulation of 16, 19; social media payment deals 17–18; social polity and 2–3; as trusted gatekeepers 3–4, 16; 24/7 news cycle and 4; veracity of information and 3–4, 8; vulnerability to fake news 4–5; *see also* journalism; traditional media
Nixon, Richard 8
Norvig, P. 6

Obama, Barack 18, 24, 67n5
online content: authentication of 9–10, 15, 29, 62, 69n21; casual consumption of 12–13; digital

literacy and 12–13; disinformation and 2, 15; filter bubbles and 15; interventions in malicious 17; manipulation of 10–12; news media and 4, 18; public uncertainty on authenticity of 29; regulation of 16–17; social media platforms and 4–5, 9–12, 17; user-generated 4–5, 11, 14, 17; widespread distribution of 4, 14–15

partisan politics 15
Peele, Jordan 24, 67n5
Pelosi, Nancy 7, 33, 38
photography: altered images and 57, 64–65; artist subject and 58; colonialism and 58; copyright law and 51; image rights and 51–53; inter-relations of text and 13; lynching 61; nonconsensual images and 58–61, 65–66, 68n15, 68n16; non-imperial 66; property rights and 51–53, 59–61, 68n16, 68n17; race and 59–61; racialized terror and 57; reality effect of images and 13; subject-turned-object in 51–52, 58–61, 66, 68n16; whiteness and 52, 57, 61, 67n8; white supremacy and 59–61; *see also* images
Pixar 57
politicians: believability of deepfake videos 6, 27, 30–31; disinformation campaigns and 29–31; synthetic audio and 7–8; targeting of female 7, 30, 33, 38
politics: deepfakes and 6–7; disinformation campaigns and 28–29, 31–32, 34; extreme partisan 15; fake news and 15, 61; influence campaigns and 29–32; participatory citizenship and 16; public trust and 16, 31, 35; shallow fakes and 7, 32
PornHub 10
pornography 25, 53, 65; *see also* fake pornography
presidential election 2016 10–12
presidential election 2020 36–37
processing fluency 27
Protection from Online Falsehoods and Manipulation Act (POFMA) 35

public trust: authenticity doubts and 31, 38; in corporate and public institutions 16; impact of deepfakes on 15, 29, 31, 34–35, 38, 41; impact of shallow fakes on 34; in news media 29, 31, 34–35, 40
puppet-master deepfakes 24
Putin, Vladimir 36

race: compositing and 57–58; digital media and 53, 55, 68n13; film industry and 51, 55, 57–58, 68n10; image construction and 51–52, 56–58; nonconsensual images and 59–61; technologies of representation and 57, 61, 65; violence and 55–56, 64, 66
reality: colonial systems and 64; deepfakes and doubt in 29; hyperreality and 13–14; manipulation of 54, 67n3; philosophy of 53; power of fiction and 55; synthetic media and 38; video representation of 13, 26
Reality Defender 9, 17
reality effect 13
Reddit 7, 10, 25, 53
Reface 37
representation: colonial systems and 64; GANs and 53; manipulation of 50; race and technologies of 57, 61; racial segregation in 57; video content and 26, 54–55; virtual communities and 16
RepresentUs 36
Respeecher 6–8
revenge porn 25
reverse imaging 28, 30, 40
Rheingold, H. 16
Rohingya Muslims 33
Roth, L. 57, 61

Sarrouf, Camille 60, 68n16
Schick, N. 38
sexual imagery 65
shallow fakes: AI technology and 7–8; in Asia 32–35; creation of 1, 7; criminal threat of 8–9; detection of 38; disinformation and 33–34; effectiveness of 7; impact on public

trust 34; influence campaigns and 32–33; information disorder and 7; labeling as deepfake 34; misinformation and 33–34; non-AI tools and 32; political use of 7, 32–33; weaponization of 33–34
Silbey, J. 12, 64
Singapore 35, 37
social media: accountability and 17; ban on fake pornography 9–10; bot networks and 33; content authentication and 10; deepfake detection and 37; disinformation campaigns and 1–2, 8, 27–30; educational deepfakes 36; face-swap tools and 25; fake news and 4; filter bubbles and 15; interventions in malicious content 10, 17; legacy news media payment deals 17–18; memes and 14; misinformation and 33–34; online news and 4, 18; protection from liability 4; shallow fakes and 33–34; synthetic profile photos and 28–30; use of free speech as defense 11–12; user-generated content 3–5, 14
social polity 2–3, 16
Solomon-Godeau, A. 65
South Korea 26, 29
spreadable media 3
Stretch, C. 11
Strubell, E. 63, 69n25
*SurSafe* 17
Suying, D. L. x
synthetic media: AI technology and 23–24; authentic video labeled as 34–35; commercialization of apps and services for 31–32; cyberattacks and 9, 41; detection of 17, 23, 28, 30; disinformation campaigns and 28; distribution of 1; educational video and 26; legitimate use of 5, 26, 38; weaponization of 35, 41; *see also* deepfakes

Taylor, Renty 59–60
technology *see* digital media
technology sector: accountability and 12; deepfake detection and 9, 37, 40; democratization of 26, 54; legislation

and 17–18, 51; neutrality of 8,
11–12; policymaking and 15–19
Telegram 25
Tencent 37
thispersondoesnotexist.com 23, 25, 39
TikTok 23, 27, 37
Tiwari, Manoj 30
traditional media *see* journalism;
news media
Truepic 69n21
Trump, Donald 10, 36, 41n5
Trusted Media Challenge 37
Turton, W. 53
Twitter 8–9, 11–12, 17, 30

Ume, Chris 37–38, 42n8
United Kingdom 4, 7, 15, 35
United Nations Interregional Crime and
Justice Research Institute 9
United States: constitutional rights
and 26; copyright law and 51;
deepfake legislation and 35;
deepfake solutions in 39; educational
deepfakes 36; election interference
in 12, 30; Facebook use in 4; fake
Facebook personas and 28; micro-
targeting of voters in 10–11; partisan
politics in 15; presidential election
2016 10–12; presidential election
2020 36–37
Unver, H. A. 15

video content: cyberattacks and 9;
deepfakes 1, 9–10; detection of 9;
face-swap 5; fake pornography 6–8,
10; forgeries 6; reality effect of 13;

shallow fakes 7; simulations and
13–14; synthetic 9
Villi, M. 4
violence: gendered 50–51, 55–56, 64;
racialized 55–56, 64, 66; shallow
fakes and 33–34
virtual reality 5, 36
visual literacy 12–13, 39–40
Visual Understanding Initiative 39

Wahl-Jorgensen, K. 8
Waldman, A. 58, 68n14
Wardle, C. 2
web-based media *see* digital media
Westerlund, M. 15
WhatsApp 30, 33
whiteness 52, 57, 61, 63, 65, 67n8
white power 65–66
white supremacy 59–61, 66
Williams, R. 55
WITNESS 39–40
women: attacks on activist 7;
cybercrime and 29; deepfake
attacks on 29–30; fake pornography
and 7–8, 50–51, 58; gendered
violence and 50–51; nonconsensual
images and 23, 58–59, 65–66;
objectification of x, 7, 50–52, 58;
sexual imagery and 65; targeting of
politicians 7, 30, 33, 38

YouTube 25

Zao 29
Zealy, Joseph 56, 59
Zuckerberg, Mark 11

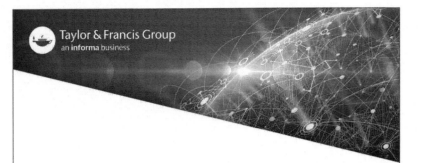

For Product Safety Concerns and Information please contact our EU
representative GPSR@taylorandfrancis.com Taylor & Francis Verlag GmbH,
Kaufingerstraße 24, 80331 München, Germany

Printed and bound by CPI Group (UK) Ltd, Croydon, CR0 4YY
11/04/2025
01844012-0003